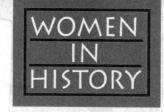

Women of the Civil Rights Movement

❧

Stuart A. Kallen

LUCENT BOOKS
An imprint of Thomson Gale, a part of The Thomson Corporation

THOMSON
✦
™
GALE

Detroit • New York • San Francisco • San Diego • New Haven, Conn. • Waterville, Maine • London • Munich

THOMSON

⸺✳⸺ ™

GALE

Cover: Demonstrators protesting segregation of students picket in
front of a school board office in St. Louis, Missouri, in 1963.

LIBRARY OF CONGRESS CATALOGING-IN-PUBLICATION DATA

Kallen, Stuart A., 1955-
  Women of the civil rights movement / by Stuart Kallen.
    p. cm. — (Women in history)
  Includes bibliographical references and index.
  ISBN 1-59018-569-2 (hard cover : alk. paper)
  1. Women civil rights workers—United States—Juvenile literature. 2. Civil rights movements—United States—History—20th century—Juvenile literature. 3. African Americans—Civil rights—History—20th century—Juvenile literature. I. Title. II. Series: Women in
history (San Diego, Calif.)
E185.61.K3385 2005
323'.0973—dc22
                                                                          2004023822

Printed in the United States of America

Contents

Foreword

The story of the past as told in traditional historical writings all too often leaves the impression that if men are not the only actors in the narrative, they are assuredly the main characters. With a few notable exceptions, males were the political, military, and economic leaders in virtually every culture throughout recorded time. Since traditional historical scholarship focuses on the public arenas of government, foreign relations, and commerce, the actions and ideas of men—or at least of powerful men—are naturally at the center of conventional accounts of the past.

In the last several decades, however, many historians have abandoned their predecessors' emphasis on "great men" to explore the past "from the bottom up," a phenomenon that has had important consequences for the study of women's history. These social historians, as they are known, focus on the day-to-day experiences of the "silent majority"—those people typically omitted from conventional scholarship because they held relatively little political or economic sway within their societies. In the new social history, members of ethnic and racial minorities, factory workers, peasants, slaves, children, and women are no longer relegated to the background but are placed at the very heart of the narrative.

Around the same time social historians began broadening their research to include women and other previously neglected elements of society, the feminist movement of the late 1960s and 1970s was also bringing unprecedented attention to the female heritage. Feminists hoped that by examining women's past experiences, contemporary women could better understand why and how gender-based expectations had developed in their societies, as well as how they might reshape inherited—and typically restrictive—economic, social, and political roles in the future.

Today, some four decades after the feminist and social history movements gave new impetus to the study of women's history, there is a rich and continually growing body of work on all aspects of women's lives in the past. The Lucent Books Women in History series draws upon this abundant and diverse literature to introduce students to women's experiences within a variety of past cultures and time periods in terms of the distinct roles they filled. In their capacities as workers, activists, and artists, women exerted significant influence on important events whether they conformed to or broke from traditional roles. The Women in History titles depict extraordinary women who managed to attain positions of influence in their male-dominated societies, including such celebrated heroines as the feisty medieval queen Eleanor of Aquitaine, the brilliant propagandist of the American Revolution Mercy Otis Warren, and the courageous African American activist of the Civil War era Harriet Tubman. Included as well are the stories of the ordinary—and often overlooked—women of the past who also helped shape their societies myriad ways—moral, intellectual, and economic—without straying far from customary gender roles: the housewives and mothers, schoolteachers and church volunteers, midwives and nurses, and wartime camp followers.

In this series, readers will discover that many of these unsung women took more significant parts in the great political and social upheavals of their day than has often been recognized. In *Women of the American Revolution,* for example, students will learn how American housewives assumed a crucial role in helping the Patriots win the war against Britain. They accomplished this by planting and harvesting fields, producing and trading goods, and doing whatever else was necessary to maintain the family farm or business in the absence of their soldier husbands despite the heavy burden of housekeeping and child-care duties they already bore. By their self-sacrificing actions, competence, and ingenuity, these anonymous heroines not only kept their families alive, but kept the economy of their struggling young nation going as well during eight long years of war.

Each volume in this series contains generous commentary from the works of respected contemporary scholars, but the Women in History series particularly emphasizes quotations from primary sources such as diaries, letters, and journals whenever possible to allow the women of the past to speak for themselves. These firsthand accounts not only help students to better understand the dimensions of women's daily spheres—the work they did, the organizations they belonged to, the physical hardships they faced—but also how they viewed themselves and their actions in the light of their society's expectations for their sex.

The distinguished American historian Mary Beard once wrote that women have always been a "force in history." It is hoped that the books in this series will help students to better appreciate the vital yet often little-known ways in which women of the past have shaped their societies and cultures.

Introduction:
Fighting for
Racial Equality

The American Civil War preserved the Union and abolished slavery, but when the war ended in 1865, the long fight for African American equal rights began. To establish the constitutional rights of former black slaves, three amendments to the Constitution were hastily ratified in the immediate postwar era. The Thirteenth Amendment abolished slavery in 1865, the Fourteenth Amendment expanded federally protected rights of black citizens in 1868, and the Fifteenth Amendment barred voting restrictions based on race in 1869. Despite these official federal protections, southern legislatures almost immediately enacted laws designed to deny African Americans civil rights, maintain the segregated status quo, and keep political and economic power in white hands. African Americans were prohibited from using train cars, restrooms, schools, parks, theaters, restaurants, and other facilities reserved for whites. Black people were discriminated against in jobs and education, in home and land ownership, and in voting

practices. The South remained a segregated society.

Segregation laws were challenged in 1892 by a black shoemaker, Homer Plessy, who objected to being forced to sit in a "Colored" railcar in Louisiana. In 1896 his case reached the U.S. Supreme Court, which ruled in the landmark *Plessy v. Ferguson* decision that separate facilities for blacks and whites were constitutional as long as they were equal. The "separate but equal" provision of the *Plessy* decision ordered states to provide black people with their own facilities. But the system of black facilities that resulted was hardly equal to that of whites. For example, southern states spent an average of ten times more money on schools for whites as they did on black schools. Most black schools were in run-down buildings with few books or supplies.

"Jump, Jim Crow"

"Separate but equal" ordinances were part of a network of discriminatory legislation known as Jim Crow laws. The name

This 1960 photo shows a segregated waiting room designated for blacks only at a bus terminal in Atlanta, Georgia.

was derived from a standard theatrical practice of the early 1800s, when black actors were not allowed to perform in theaters attended by whites. Instead, white actors in blackface makeup performed roles of black characters. In 1831, a white singer painted his face black and sang a song called "Jump, Jim Crow," and the name quickly became associated with segregation.

Throughout the first half of the twentieth century, African Americans were forced to endure the indignity of the "separate but equal" policy throughout the South. Black civil rights organizations, such as the National Association for the Advancement of Colored People (NAACP), founded in 1909, fought segregation, but change was incremental. Even after millions of Americans bravely fought to bring democracy to Western Europe and Japan in World War II, black veterans returned home to a divided society, denied the most basic rights guaranteed by the Constitution.

This situation began to slowly change in the 1940s when President Franklin Roosevelt signed the Fair Employment order to fight discrimination against African Americans in the job market. In 1944, the NAACP won a long court fight to have white-only election primaries rendered illegal. (This allowed black people to vote in the South Carolina primaries for the first time since 1877.) In 1948, President Harry Truman desegregated the military. These advances, however, did little to change the life of the average African American in the South or in the urban industrial centers of the North, where many southern blacks sought work after World War II.

Striking a Blow Against Jim Crow

It was not until May 17, 1954, that the first major blow against Jim Crow was struck by the United States Supreme Court. In the historic case of *Brown v. Board of Education of Topeka, Kansas,* the Court ruled that separate facilities for blacks were inherently unequal and therefore unconstitutional. The *Brown* decision stated: "To separate the Negro children from others of a similar age and qualifications solely because of their race generates a feeling of inferiority as to their

In 1956 National Guardsmen maintain order as black children wait to enter an all-white elementary school in Clay, Kentucky.

Women of the Civil Rights Movement

status in the community that may affect their hearts and minds in a way unlikely ever to be undone."[1] Two weeks later, the Supreme Court ordered all seventeen states with "separate but equal" primary and secondary schools to integrate them immediately. In 1955, the courts expanded the ruling to apply to tax-supported colleges and universities as well.

Brown v. Board of Education set off the most divisive unrest since the Civil War. The governors of South Carolina, Georgia, and Mississippi threatened to abolish public schools before they would let blacks and whites attend classes together. One hundred senators and congressmen from the South signed a petition against the ruling. Racist hate groups formed to protest the decision. State, county, and city politicians drew up laws to circumvent the Supreme Court ruling, and the courtroom victory did little to help integrate schools. To counter the opposition to segregation, African American activists and their supporters filed more lawsuits and organized boycotts, sit-ins, and protest marches.

As segregationists battled black protesters on the streets and in the courts, little changed for average African Americans. In 1960, 99 percent of southern black children continued to attend segregated schools. And no African American high school graduates were allowed to attend white colleges in the South. In the North and West, as well as the South,

schools attended by African Americans were overcrowded and underfunded. Dismal conditions led to high dropout rates, and in cities such as Cleveland and Los Angeles, up to 70 percent of inner-city African Americans did not graduate from high school. African Americans were once again shown that noble words on paper could not change the reality of the discrimination they faced daily.

The Double Handicap

The burdens of racism and discrimination fell particularly hard upon African American women, who were overwhelmingly poor. Many were unemployed, and those who found work were often paid inadequate wages to perform menial work. Inner-city black communities suffered as whites abandoned cities for suburbs in the 1950s and took the tax base with them. Grocery stores in black neighborhoods were boarded up, parks fell to ruin, and city schools sank to substandard conditions. And since women were responsible for feeding, tending, and educating children, they were most affected by these deficient conditions.

Black women faced extra hardships: They not only encountered prejudice because of their race but also were discriminated against because of their gender. As civil rights leader Mary Church Terrell said, "We labor under the double handicap of race and sex."[2] Even powerful male African American leaders failed to see the abilities of black women. As the nationally recognized black nationalist leader Malcolm X wrote in *The Autobiography of Malcolm X:* "[The] true nature of man is to be strong, and a woman's true nature is to be weak, and while a man must at all times respect his woman, at the same time he needs to understand that he must control her if he expects to get her respect."[3]

Although women were strong supporters of Malcolm X and other civil rights leaders, they were expected to remain silent about sexism within the civil rights movement. Many men, and some women, felt that discussions of the black woman's place in society distracted from the main goals of the civil rights movement such as integrating public institutions, ensuring voting rights, and ending unequal treatment in the job and housing markets. Women's issues were barely addressed as Dorothy Height, founder of the National Council of Negro Women (NCNW), writes: "Though every statistic showed us that a number of our families were headed by women, we were still dominated by the view that if men were given enough, the women would be better off. There was not that sense of equal partnership."[4]

In this environment, male civil rights leaders often treated women as inferiors, expecting them to make coffee, paint signs, and do secretarial work while the men worked with politicians, lawyers, and other professionals. Despite the rampant sexism, women played many roles in the civil rights movement. They were organizers, protesters, educators, orators, fundraisers, and leaders. They participated in sit-ins and marches where they were beaten and jailed. By the late sixties some women became Black Power radicals and militants, preaching revolution and the violent overthrow of white society. Others joined the mainstream, running for political office and fighting for equal rights on the national stage. Throughout the fight, women authors, singers, and actors found creative ways to express the joys and frustrations of the era.

The civil rights movement reached its zenith in the 1960s and early 1970s when landmark legislation finally overturned centuries of institutionalized racism. Although many feel that the fight for equality is not over, the women of the civil rights movement who fought violence, hatred, and oppression between 1945 and 1975 laid the groundwork for other campaigns for equal rights, including the modern feminist movement and Hispanic and Native American rights movements. In their various roles as fighters and organizers, the women of the civil rights movement made racism and discrimination unacceptable while charting a new course for the nation and the world.

Chapter 1:
Women in Civil Rights Organizations

From its earliest days, the civil rights movement was driven by grassroots organizations that effectively influenced politicians, publicized civil rights issues, sponsored demonstrations and legal defenses, and mobilized people to participate in various forms of nonviolent protest. Women played active roles in the founding and guiding of these organizations, and they also did the hard work of keeping them running in the face of sometimes overwhelming opposition.

The public face of the most prominent organizations—the National Association for the Advancement of Colored People (NAACP), the Student Nonviolent Coordinating Committee (SNCC), and the Southern Christian Leadership Conference (SCLC)—was mostly male. Likewise, organized religion played a vital role in the civil rights movement, but in churches, at a time when women were not allowed to be ordained ministers, men held positions of authority. As Steven F. Lawson writes in *Civil Rights Crossroads*:

Whether they were ministers or secular leaders of civil rights organizations, men commanded the bulk of the publicity devoted to coverage of the freedom struggle. . . . This hardly comes as a surprise because during the postwar era affairs of state and matters of public policy were seen as resting predominantly in male hands. . . . [The] male heads of the preeminent civil rights groups served as spokesmen for the protests and, in turn, attracted most of the limelight.[5]

It was women, however, whose efforts helped keep the black churches strong. As historians Darlene Clarke Hine and Kathleen Thompson state: "Men stood in the pulpit and sat on the church board. Women did everything else."[6] "Everything else" included acting as fund-raisers and volunteers to head church choirs, youth groups, missionary societies, and day care programs. Women were also the rank and file of the secular organizations that made up the civil rights movement. According

Although men, like Martin Luther King Jr., were the most prominent civil rights leaders, many women, like Coretta Scott King (in white hat), were just as active in the movement.

to Lawson, without the "support [women] provided, the movement would have never gotten off the ground."[7]

The Women's Political Council

Some women devoted themselves first to local organizations, motivated by personal victimization within the segregationist South. A noteworthy example is that of Mary Fair Burks, a chairperson of the English department at Alabama State College in Montgomery. In 1946, Burks, an African American, was involved in an automobile accident with another vehicle driven by a white woman. Burks was immediately arrested when a bystander falsely accused her of cursing the other driver. She was roughly interrogated and only released when a witness exonerated her. Humiliated by the experience, Burk founded the Women's Political Council (WPC) of Montgomery. As WPC leader Jo Ann Gibson Robinson states:

The WPC was formed for the purpose of inspiring Negroes to live above mediocrity, to elevate their thinking, to fight juvenile and adult delinquency, to register and vote, and in general to improve their status as a group. We were "women power," organized to cope with any injustice, no matter what, against [African Americans].[8]

The original membership of the WPC was mainly composed of Burks's contemporaries, middle-class black women who lived or worked near Alabama State College: schoolteachers, college professors, supervisors, principals, social workers, nurses, and other community workers. Burk limited membership to one hundred people and purposely excluded men because, she said, "they would take it over and women wouldn't be able to do what they could do."[9]

The women of the WPC used their training and expertise to further the twin goals of registering voters and instructing high school students in political activism. WPC members used a novel approach in instructing teenage girls: To increase their confidence in the roles of politicians and train them in legislative and administrative processes, they staged mock elections and held mock government sessions. Some of those who participated in these performances grew up to become lawyers, politicians, and judges themselves.

Applications to join the WPC quickly exceeded the group's original membership limit. To accommodate more women in the popular organization, two additional chapters were formed in Montgomery. Each had its own president, secretary, treasurer, and telephone coordinator, but chapter presidents met often to coordinate activities, which expanded to include advocacy for people who had experienced racial discrimination.

WPC secretaries fielded telephone complaints about police brutality, and WPC officials met with Montgomery's mayor and city commissioners to alleviate problems, such as racist bus drivers, associated with Montgomery's segregated bus system. They lobbied city administrators to hire black bus drivers for black neighborhoods, and they rallied, unsuccessfully, against segregationist seating policies. Members also attended city council meetings when issues important to the minority community were discussed.

Although the WPC had a good working relationship with the white politicians who ran Montgomery, they had little success in ending racist policies. Then in 1955, the good relations became adversarial when WPC gave its strong support to the black community's citywide bus boycott, which eventually paralyzed city services. This yearlong boycott, one of the most significant events of the civil rights movement, is credited with finally changing the status quo and integrating the city's buses.

In the Trenches with the NAACP

During the 1940s and 1950s, when the WPC played an important role in Montgomery race relations, the National Association for the Advancement of Colored People operated as the foremost civil rights organization on a national level. Like the WPC, the NAACP membership was mostly middle-class African Americans, including many teachers, ministers, rabbis, and professionals. Unlike the Montgomery-based operation, however, the association had both male and female members.

Two women, Ida Wells-Barnett and Mary White Ovington, were among the six founders of the NAACP in 1909. Ovington was known for her fund-raising abilities and her leadership roles during the stormy early years of the organization. When she was elected chairman of the board and director of all NAACP branches in 1919, Ovington was known as the "Mother of the New Emancipation."

By the 1940s the NAACP was active in nearly every state and was known for attracting strong female organizers. Ella Baker was one such woman who began working with the group as a field organizer, earning twenty-nine dollars a week to visit cities and towns of all sizes in the Deep South to raise funds to recruit new members. In a 1971 interview, Baker described her role in the association:

> I used to leave New York [City] about the 15th of February and travel through the South for four or five months. I would go to, say, Birmingham, Alabama and help to organize membership campaigns. . . . You would deal with whatever the local problem was, and on the basis of the needs of the people you would try to organize them in the NAACP.[10]

Birmingham was one of the most virulently racist cities in the South. Blacks had referred to it as "Bombingham" since the late 1940s because local segregationists called "night riders" terrorized the community by tossing explosives onto the porches of black families and activists. In this atmosphere, Baker and other field-workers such as Lucille Black and Charlotte Crump risked their lives by recruiting members for the NAACP. Such work was considered a radical act by racists who would do almost anything to stop integration and intimidate black citizens.

Despite the dangers, Baker pursued a new strategy for the NAACP that took her into some of the most poverty-stricken neighborhoods. Instead of relying on funds from middle-class blacks and white liberals, Baker recruited average black cit-

Inside and Outside the Home

❧

Women's activism in civil rights organizations was often a natural outgrowth of their involvement in churches. According to Steven F. Lawson in *Civil Rights Crossroads*, activism also grew out of the roles women naturally played within the home:

> Women not only sustained the community through religious and social activities, they also nurtured the civil rights struggle in their familial roles as wives and mothers. . . . Because the struggle relied on young people as plaintiffs in education cases and as marchers in demonstrations, women

had enormous influence in shaping their children's decision to join the cause. It took great courage and faith to put their daughters' and sons' lives in jeopardy in the face of often brutal white resistance. Both inside and outside the home, women played an essential part in building the foundation for the movement to flourish. Depicting women as organizers, however, does not do justice to the leadership they exhibited. They did not usually hold official titles or follow formal job descriptions, but operating behind the scenes in routine, often gendered ways.

izens in the all-male domains of inner-city barbershops, pool halls, shoe shine stands, and bars. Although it was considered controversial for a well-bred woman to enter such places in the 1940s, Baker made her point with sarcasm, saying she had a "strong desire to place the NAACP and its programs on the lips of all the people . . . the uncouth MASSES included."[11]

Recognized for her hard work and successful recruitment of new members, Baker was made assistant field secretary for the NAACP in 1941 and became the national director of branches in 1943.

Although this new role made her the highest-ranking woman in the organization, with influence over national policy, Baker preferred the grassroots approach to organizing: "[Persons] living and working in a community are in a better position to select leadership for a community project than one coming into the community."[12] This belief led to clashes with the male leadership of the NAACP, who concerned themselves with larger issues. Barbara Ransby explains in *Ella Baker and the Black Freedom Movement*: "[As] the predominantly male spokespersons for black America made pronouncements about . . . federal legislation and world affairs, organizers like Ella Baker were fighting in the trenches of southern battlefields for social and economic justice for African Americans."[13] Baker's coworker Daisy Lampkin put it more succinctly: "Our male leadership is so busy with their private interests that nothing is done unless the women do it."[14]

Ella Baker worked tirelessly to recruit average black citizens to the NAACP and became the highest-ranking woman in the organization in 1943.

Facing Gender Bias

Women continued to fight both racism and sexism in organizations where gender bias was common and men made most of the important decisions. This was no less the case in the Southern Christian Leadership Conference, founded in 1958. Its director, the Reverend Dr. Martin Luther King Jr., was a charismatic and nationally recognized minister known for oratory featuring eloquent pleas for tolerance and cooperation. Nonetheless, although women played successful roles in many civil rights protests initiated by the SCLC, the upper ranks of the council were staffed by male ministers. As J. Douglas Allen-Taylor writes on the "Septima Clark: Teacher to a Movement" Web site: "Many of the preachers who made up SCLC's ruling corps were used to women taking a back seat in their churches and in their homes, and they did not look lightly on a woman taking a leadership role in their organization."[15]

Baker, who helped organize the SCLC in its early years, offered her opinion as to why she would never play a leadership role in the council:

First, I'm a woman. Also, I'm not a minister. . . . Also . . . the problem of being a woman, and an older woman [age fifty-six in 1959] presents some problems. Number one, I was old enough to be the mother of the leadership. The combination of the basic attitude of men, and especially ministers, as to what the role of women in their church setups is—that of taking orders, not providing leadership.[16]

In this environment, women were only allowed to participate in education and fund-raising programs. Black civil rights activist Septima Clark, who was born in South Carolina in 1898 and had been a member of the NAACP since 1919, observed this gender bias firsthand. As head of the council's Citizenship School movement, Clark educated thousands of community leaders from 1957 to 1970. Although civil rights leader Andrew Young Jr., the top aide to Martin Luther King, said the Citizenship Education Program was "the base on which the whole civil rights movement was built,"[17] Clark was prevented from attending SCLC executive committee meetings, and the council's high-profile publicity department rarely credited Clark for her work. She later wrote about her experiences:

I was on the Executive Staff of SCLC, but the men on it didn't listen to me too well. They liked to send me into many places, because I could always make a path in to get people to listen to what I have to say. But those

men didn't have any faith in women, none whatsoever. They just thought that women were sex symbols and had no contribution to make.[18]

These attitudes prevailed even though marginalizing women compromised an organization's fund-raising ability. The situation faced by Carole Hoover, special projects director for the SCLC in 1962, is an example. Hoover tried to discuss council business with King, but her requests were repeatedly ignored. Hoover was forced to explain her feelings in a letter to King:

I am so obviously excluded from meetings where programming, policy and future plans for the organization are dealt with. Consequently, I am poorly informed, which is bad, because I am constantly before groups for promotions, fund raising and other things where it is mandatory to be equipped with information on the present program.... I feel that if I am to remain on the staff at least I should be informed.[19]

For many women within the SCLC, being excluded from executive meetings was the least of their problems. While facing gender bias from within, several were targets of violence from enemies of the civil rights movement. In Dawson, Georgia, someone fired thirty rounds with an automatic rifle into the home of African American Citizenship School teacher Carolyn Daniels, who was hit in the foot. While hospitalized, Daniels's home was destroyed by a bomb. In Williamson, North Carolina, SCLC activist Sarah Small was hit, cursed, and thrown against a police car when she attempted to integrate her local library.

The Student Nonviolent Coordinating Committee

Gender bias within the ranks of mainstream civil rights organizations caused some women—even women who served in higher positions in the mainstream organizations—to seek out more inclusive organizations. For example, Diane Nash, a black Chicago native, the youth group coordinator for the SCLC, and one of the few women allowed to participate in the SCLC conventions, left the council for the Student Nonviolent Coordinating Committee in 1960. SNCC was a political organization formed in 1960 by black college students dedicated to banning segregation in the South and giving young African Americans their own voice in the civil rights movement. While King and other leaders hoped SNCC would act as the youth wing of the SCLC, the student group remained fiercely independent, favoring democracy, personal empowerment, and consensus rather than hier-

archy and authority because, as Baker says, "strong people don't need strong leaders."[20]

Baker was instrumental in nurturing the group, providing work space for the committee in her SCLC office, and allowing the students to use copy machines and other office equipment. And with a woman as powerful as Baker acting as a guiding force within the organization, it is not surprising that women had a strong presence in SNCC. They played key roles in the organization, were involved equally in decision making, and spoke publicly for the group. African American history professor Charles Payne explains:

[In] SNCC's early years, women were always involved in the development of policy and the execution of the group's program. The group was ... willing to work with anyone who was willing to have them, traditional considerations of status notwithstanding. They worked with sharecroppers as well as doctors, with the pool room crowd as well as the church crowd. SNCC organizers emphasized finding and developing nontraditional sources of leadership. Women obviously represented an enormous pool of untapped leadership potential. Much of SNCC's organizing activity in the [largely

Violent Reprisals Against Women

A❧

Although black women were customarily treated with a slightly higher degree of respect than men in the segregationist South, this situation did not apply to African American women civil rights organizers. In *Women in the Civil Rights Movement*, African American history professor Charles Payne explains why:

Reprisals against women in the rural South were constant and highly visible. Examination of [records] suggests that some of the most violent incidents of reprisals took place against women. Women who were even rumored to be part of the movement lost their jobs. Every adult woman I interviewed got fired, except for those who quit because they expected to get fired. Women were regularly clubbed at demonstrations or beaten in jail. The homes of women activists were regularly shot into. . . . Moreover, it is misleading to think of reprisals as being directed against merely the individual who was involved. Anyone who joined the movement placed his or her whole family at risk. When one person got evicted, the entire family was evicted. . . . The [racist] Citizen's Council in particular made it a point to put pressure on the entire family. If anyone in a family was known to be a part of the movement, every adult in that family was likely to have trouble finding work or getting credit. Similarly, the most popular forms of violence in that period—arson, drive-by shootings into homes, and bombings—were reprisals against family units, not individuals.

black Mississippi Delta region between Jackson and Natchez] involved door-to-door canvassing, which meant that women were as likely as men to encounter organizers. SNCC, despite the traditional definitions of sex roles held by many of its members, was structurally open to female participation in a way that many older organizations were not. Had SNCC employed a more traditional style of organizing—working primarily through previously established leadership—it might not have achieved the degree of female participation it did.[21]

In addition to being "woman friendly," SNCC was also a young organization, with 75 percent of its field-workers under the age of twenty-two. Some of these young women helped galvanize a national student

Young black women in the SNCC like these marching in Washington, D.C., in 1963 inspired a generation of young activists to take up the civil rights struggle.

movement, as described on the "Student Nonviolent Coordinating Committee" Web site:

> As SNCC "freedom fighters" became deeply involved in an expanding southern freedom movement, they developed a distinctive style of representative protest that inspired many black southerners. . . . A willingness to challenge powerful institutions allowed SNCC organizers to be particularly effective in the most racially repressive regions of the Black Belt. . . . SNCC workers became role models for a generation of young activists, both inside and outside the South, who challenged many of the assumptions that perpetuated injustice and oppression in American society.[22]

"Connective Tissue"

Although most of the women who worked for SNCC were black southerners, some northern blacks, like Diane Nash, moved south to join the group. Between 1960 and 1965 about 350 northern and southern white women, many of them Jewish, also worked for SNCC and other civil rights organizations. In general, the white women worked in support roles such as fund-raising, media relations, and communications. Roberta Galler, a Jewish civil rights activist, is one such woman. She stayed in her hometown of Chicago to publish the student journal *New University Thought*, which reported news from the southern civil rights movement. Galler also hosted SNCC fund-raisers where civil rights activists told harrowing stories of beatings and death threats received while working for integration in the South.

Galler's involvement was more than scholarly. Through her contacts with SNCC workers, she took on the role of care provider, opening her home to feed and support civil rights activists recovering from the mental strain and physical injuries incurred during SNCC campaigns. Debra L. Schultz further explains Galler's roles in SNCC in *Going South: Jewish Women in the Civil Rights Movement*:

> Keeping in close touch with SNCC field offices on a daily basis, Galler made direct interventions that brought food, information, money, national attention, and personal support to SNCC centers across the South. Movements for radical social change (and organizations like

SNCC) generally fight against great odds with limited resources. Women like Galler manage, protect, and preserve precious human and material resources. They function as connective tissue—taking care of people's needs.[23]

While Galler used her connections in the North to support the movement, other women gave up middle-class comforts to fight for racial equality in the South. Dorothy Miller, for example, quit a secure job and left her apartment in Manhattan to work for SNCC in Atlanta. Starting out as a poorly paid typist, Miller soon took on the role of author and editor, working on articles for the SNCC newspaper *Student Voice*. The paper was extremely important, one of the only journals in the nation that reported on the constant violence perpetrated on African Americans and civil rights activists. As Schultz writes: "Miller helped bring the reality of southern violence to national attention."[24]

Miller also took on the roles of a publicist, advocate, and media spokesperson, writing and submitting press releases about the arrest and mistreatment of demonstrators to Atlanta newspapers and television and radio stations. In addition, Miller gave radio interviews about civil rights events and wrote telegrams to federal officials at the Department of Justice,

"My Whole World Was Expanded"

❧

Throughout the fifties and sixties, men were the main officeholders in most civil rights organizations. Many women experienced joy from their roles in the movement, however, because speaking out against racism and injustice was empowering in and of itself. Bernice Johnson Reagon makes this point in *How Long? How Long?* by Belinda Robnett when speaking about her years in the Student Nonviolent Coordinating Committee (SNCC) in the 1960s:

> One of the things that happened to me through SNCC was [that] my whole world was expanded in terms of what

I could do as a person. I'm describing an unleashing of my potential as an empowered human being. I never experienced being held back. I only experienced being challenged and searching within myself to see if I had the courage to do what came up in my mind. And I think if you talked to a lot of people who participated in the movement, who were in SNCC, you find women describing themselves being pushed in ways they had never experienced before. . . . I was challenged to go further than I'd ever gone before. And to that extent, it was an incredible experience.

in Washington, D.C., urging protection of SNCC protesters. Schultz describes the importance of Miller's work: "With such effective representations of movement work, designed to elicit legal, moral, and financial support, SNCC was able to rise to national prominence quickly."[25]

"I Just Thought They Were Wrong"

While women like Miller worked mostly behind the scenes, a few white women, such as Sandra "Casey" Cason, were full-time staff members of SNCC. The *Min-*

neapolis Tribune described Cason somewhat dismissively as a "beautiful . . . coed with honey blond hair and a southern voice so soft it would not startle a boll weevil,"[26] but her controversial lifestyle flew in the face of traditional feminine norms. For example, while attending the University of Texas at Austin in 1960, Cason lived with a group called the Christian Faith-and-Life Community. With black and white people living together, this was one of the few integrated places in the South. In an era when a fourteen-year-old African American,

Emmett Till, was murdered for allegedly whistling at a white woman, Cason acknowledged that she "was not acting the way a Southern girl was expected to act. . . . [Most] people thought I should not associate with blacks, particularly not black men [but I] just thought they were wrong."[27]

Cason's activism in the student civil rights movement brought her to a meeting in Minneapolis of the National Student Association (NSA), where she took on the role of orator. Cason and others were seeking NSA backing of SNCC demonstrations, which the NSA refused to endorse, fearing that protests such as sit-ins at segregated lunch counters would result in violence. Hoping to convince the NSA to give financial backing and nationwide campus support to SNCC, Cason gave a speech, stating:

I cannot say to a person who suffers injustice, "Wait." . . . Perhaps you can. I can't. And having decided that I cannot urge caution, I must stand with [that person]. If I had known that not a single lunch counter would open as a result of my action, I could not have done differently. If I had known that violence would result, I would not have done differently than I did.[28]

Cason's speech electrified the crowd, and the NSA voted overwhelmingly to support SNCC. Another white supporter, Connie Curry, later said: "There is no question . . . that [Cason's speech] was a personal turning point for many of the white delegates and probably a decisive moment in the history of NSA's civil rights activism."[29]

Cason's work, like that of so many others, was performed for the most unselfish reasons. With a common goal of integrating society, white and black women worked together to convince a nation to live up to its moral obligations and banish segregation forever.

Chapter 2:
Protesting Segregation

❦

African Americans challenged Jim Crow laws in city, state, and federal courts throughout the first half of the twentieth century. While there were a few legal victories, the decisions of judges had little practical effect on the entrenched segregation of the South. Those interested in keeping racist laws in place controlled newspapers and local and state governments, and worked in police, sheriff, and highway patrol departments. They were backed by members of vigilante hate groups such as the Ku Klux Klan, which resorted to terrorist tactics such as beatings, bombings, and shootings whenever African Americans demanded equal rights. In 1955 in Belzoni, Mississippi, for example, Klan members shot African American minister George Lee, who had encouraged other black citizens to vote. The sheriff refused to investigate the case. Similar incidents occurred in hundreds of rural southern towns for decades. These events were rarely covered by the national press.

Less violent than the Klan but equally harmful were public organizations called White Citizens' Councils. The councils fought segregation without violence, using state and city laws to repress African Americans. Citizens' Councils were often made up of the most "respectable" people in the community, including law enforcement officers. Their main weapon was economic power. For example, in 1960 a local newspaper in Yazoo, Mississippi, ran an ad that printed the names, addresses, and phone numbers of blacks who had signed a petition asking local school boards to integrate the schools. The people who held jobs lost them. Their credit was cut off at local banks. Of the fifty-three people who signed the petition, fifty-one took their names off. Still, they did not get their jobs back. The situation was similar in other small southern towns.

"Tired of Giving In"

Beaten, intimidated, ignored, and murdered for decades, African Americans needed only a catalyst to turn building resentment into mass protest. The galvanizing

In 1955 Rosa Parks (pictured in the aisle seat of an integrated bus in 1956) refused to surrender her seat on a Montgomery, Alabama, bus to a white man, sparking the Mongomery bus boycott.

moment came on the evening of December 1, 1955, when a neatly dressed forty-two-year-old black woman named Rosa Parks boarded a city bus in Montgomery, Alabama, for a ride home from work. Parks walked to the back of the bus and took a seat just behind the section marked "Whites Only." After a long day as a tailor's assistant, she was glad to sit down. As the bus wound its way through town, it filled up with passengers until every seat in the "Whites Only" section was taken. Two more white men boarded the bus. The driver yelled over his shoulder for the first two rows of blacks to move back.

After a few minutes, three black people rose and stood in the aisle. Rosa Parks, her lap covered with packages and her feet aching, refused to move. The driver shouted at her to get up. Parks would not budge. Although most accounts of the incident report that she was too weary to move because of a long day at work, Parks herself later said, "The only tired I was, was tired of giving in."[30] At this moment, Parks became a civil rights protester, a decision she did not make lightly, as she recalls:

> As I sat there, I tried not to think about what might happen. I knew that anything was possible. I could be manhandled or beaten. I could be arrested. People have asked me if it occurred

Riding the Bus with Jim Crow

Although Rosa Parks is credited with instigating the Montgomery bus boycott, members of the Women's Political Council had long protested treatment of black citizens on public transportation. In *The Montgomery Bus Boycott and the Women Who Started It*, Jo Ann Gibson Robinson presented a list of protest points she delivered to Montgomery city commissioners in early 1955:

Among the things itemized in our protest were:

1. Continuous discourtesies with obscene language, especially name-calling in addressing black patrons.

2. Buses stopped at each block in neighborhoods where whites lived, but at every two blocks or block and a half in black neighborhoods.

3. Bus drivers' requirement that Negro passengers pay fares at the front of the bus, then step down . . . and walk to the back door to board the bus. . . . In many instances the driver drove away before the patrons who had paid at the front could board the bus from the rear.

4. That the front ten double seats on each bus (out of a total seating for thirty-six) were reserved for whites, whether there were enough whites riding the bus to occupy them or not. Even when no whites were aboard, those seats were reserved, just in case one or two did ride. In many instances black riders had to stand over those empty seats.

to me then that I could be the test case the NAACP had been looking for [to challenge segregation on public transportation]. I did not think about that at all. In fact if I had let myself think too deeply about what might happen to me, I might have gotten off the bus. But I chose to remain.[31]

Parks was arrested and thrown in jail for violating Montgomery segregation laws. Not only were blacks forced to sit at the back of the bus in a separate section, but the law also stated that blacks had to surrender the "Colored" seats to whites if the buses were full. This policy was enforced even though there were forty thousand black bus riders and only twelve thousand white riders.

Parks was not the first black woman in Montgomery to protest this injustice. In March 1955, a fifteen-year-old named Claudette Colvin had refused to give up her seat and was dragged, kicking and screaming, from the bus by police. Eighteen-year-old Louise Smith had a similar experience in October 1955. Parks's refusal to move, however, set off the Montgomery bus boycott, an unprecedented protest that took on great symbolic significance and would have important consequences.

"My Soul Is Free"

Many members of the Women's Political Council had been contemplating a bus boycott for years. The day after the Parks arrest, they went into action, printing more than fifty thousand fliers that announced a one-day boycott on Monday, December 5. Professor Jo Ann Gibson Robinson of Alabama State College wrote the copy for the notice. To avoid confrontation with college administrators, she visited the college after midnight to make copies of the flier in her office. It read, in part:

Another Negro woman has been arrested and thrown in jail because she refused to get up out of her seat on the bus for a white person to sit down. . . . This has to be stopped. Negroes have rights, too, for if Negroes did not ride the buses, they could not operate. Three-fourths of the riders are Negroes, yet we are arrested, or have to stand over empty seats. If we do not do something to stop these arrests, they will continue.

The next time it may be you, or your daughter, or mother. . . . We are, therefore, asking every Negro to stay off the buses Monday in protest of the arrest and trial. Don't ride the buses to work, to town, to school, or anywhere on Monday. You can afford to stay out of school for one day if you have no other way to go except by bus. You can also afford to stay out of town for one day. If you work, take a cab, or walk. But please, children and grown-ups, don't ride the bus at all on Monday.[32]

After the fliers were printed, more than a dozen women of the WPC took on the role of distributors and delivery persons. They loaded their cars with large bundles of notices and delivered them to other women who hand-distributed them to their neighborhood churches, schools, beauty parlors, taverns, factories, and other community gathering spots within reach of nearly every black person in Montgomery. By two o'clock the next afternoon, the protest was announced, and as Robinson writes, "No one knew where the notices had come from or who had arranged for their circulation, and no one cared. . . . But deep within the heart of every black person was a joy he or she dared not reveal."[33]

While most people were willing to keep news of the boycott secret until

December 5 to avoid conflict with police and racist hate groups, not everyone was happy with the protest. On December 2, one black woman who worked as a maid became an informer, turning over the boycott notice to her white employers, who immediately notified the bus company, city government officials, and the police. That afternoon, full coverage of the boycott appeared in Montgomery's two local newspapers, two television stations, and four radio stations. Rather than hurt the cause, however, the informer only served to spread news of the boycott and unify the resolve of the city's black community.

On Monday December 5, the buses were empty. Montgomery's eighteen black-owned taxi companies agreed to transport people for the same fare as the bus—ten cents. Although there were not enough taxis and some protesters were forced to walk miles to work, some felt liberated for the first time. One woman who walked halfway across town was asked by a minister if she was tired. She replied: "Well, my body may be a bit tired, but for many years now my soul has been tired. Now my soul is resting. So I don't mind if my body is tired, because my soul is free."[34]

The one-day Montgomery boycott turned into a permanent protest. For the next thirteen months, empty buses rolled through the streets of Montgomery. The boycott also made Martin Luther King Jr. famous as he emerged as a spokesman for black civil rights. Although King got most of the credit when the Supreme Court struck down the Montgomery bus laws on December 20, 1956, the boycott would never have been initially successful without the women protesters who were there at the beginning. And their techniques were soon imitated when similar boycotts were organized in Birmingham; Tallahassee, Florida; and other southern cities. Many felt, however, that the boycotts were only the first step in ending institutionalized racism. When Parks was asked how she felt about the victory, she replied: "It didn't feel like a victory, actually. There still had to be a great deal to do."[35]

Jail-No-Bail

Parks was referring to other segregationist policies in the South that remained in place even as the buses were integrated. Lunch counters, for example, were still segregated, and African Americans were unable to eat in many downtown areas. In *Too Heavy a Load* Deborah Gray White explains how segregated lunch counters hurt black women:

Segregation, with its prohibitions . . . denied black women basic dignity. Finding ways of telling hungry children why they could not eat or drink at restaurants and soda foun-

A young white man dumps sugar on the heads of protesters staging a sit-in at a segregated lunch counter at Woolworth's in Jackson, Mississippi, in 1963.

tains was almost as trying as riding the segregated buses that extended the oppression of the black domestic's workday.[36]

African Americans began to protest lunch counter segregation on February 1, 1960, when four neatly dressed black college students entered the Woolworth's department store in Greensboro, South Carolina. The store had a lunch counter that catered to whites only, and as Zita Allen writes in *Black Women Leaders of the Civil Rights Movement*, this was an "inhu-

mane and humiliating daily [reminder] of the belief that blacks were inferior to whites."[37] When the students sat down and ordered coffee, the waitress refused to serve them. They sat quietly at the counter until the store closed an hour later.

Although the first four protesters were men, news of the sit-in spread quickly through local African American college campuses. The next day, twenty black students, both male and female, sat at the lunch counter. On the third day, sixty students were refused service. Taking on the role of nonviolent protester required personal courage, however, even as the numbers swelled. The students were harshly taunted by huge crowds of white men that showered them with broken eggs, hot coffee, ketchup, and lit cigarettes while police watched from a distance. Despite this abuse, lunch counter sit-ins spread to sixty-eight cities in the following months.

At a February sit-in in Rock Hill, South Carolina, police decided to arrest more than eighty protesters for disorderly conduct. For many of the female college students this was a terrifying experience, as Lynne Olson writes in *Freedom's Daughters:* "Only bad people went to jail, [they] had been taught, and bad things happened to them once they were there."[38] These bad things included being packed so tightly into filthy, overcrowded cells that no one could sit or lie down, and being served food that was cut with sawdust and coffee that was mixed with salt instead of sugar. Worse, women were strip-searched, sexually harassed, and sometimes raped by white male police officers.

Civil rights protesters were commonly fined about fifty dollars or thirty days in jail for disorderly conduct. While most paid the fine, Diane Nash and Doris Ruby Smith decided to serve thirty days behind bars instead. Nash told the judge why she was willing to take on the role of political prisoner: "We feel that if we pay these fines we would be contributing to and supporting injustice and immoral practices that have been performed in the arrest and conviction of the defendants."[39] Nash's "jail-no-bail" protest was quickly adopted by sit-in demonstrators throughout the South. Soon local jails were overflowing with protesters, creating a huge workload for guards and police who had to tend to their basic needs.

Nash's brave stand propelled her to the forefront of the protest movement. Her pictures appeared in newspapers, on television, and on the cover of *Jet*, a magazine with a large African American readership. Nash was uncomfortable in the glare of the media spotlight, however, and her celebrity made her the focus of racists who singled her out at protests. Nash expressed self-doubt about her role:

[White] people down here are mean. . . . [Not only that] we are . . . coming up against white Southern men who are forty and fifty and sixty years old, who are politicians and judges and owners of businesses, and I am twenty-two years old. What am I doing? And how is this little group of students my age going to stand up to these powerful people?[40]

Despite such doubts, the courage and dedication of the women who joined the ranks of sit-in protesters soon paid off. Widespread public pressure compelled the government to condemn segregation, while widespread negative publicity forced Woolworth's to change company policy to allow integrated lunch counters. While many lunch counters remained segregated in smaller towns, this was an inspirational victory for black activists and provided a turning point in the civil rights movement.

Facing Violence for Freedom Rides

In 1961, after sit-ins ended segregation at lunch counters, protesters turned their attention to bus stations throughout the South, where restrooms and waiting rooms were marked by signs that said "Whites Only" and "Colored Only." Although this practice was outlawed by a 1960 Supreme Court decision that banned segregation in interstate train and

In 1961 a busload of Freedom Riders leaves Montgomery under the protection of the National Guard after having been assaulted when they arrived in the city.

Protesting Segregation: The Routes of the Freedom Riders

The Freedom Riders were groups of civil rights activists who traveled by bus through the South in 1961 to protest illegal segregation practices. They encountered hostility and violence along the way, but by year's end, through public pressure, they had succeeded in strengthening desegregation laws.

Newark

NEW JERSEY

DELAWARE

MARYLAND

ILLINOIS

INDIANA

OHIO

WEST VIRGINIA

Washington, D.C.

St. Louis

MISSOURI

KENTUCKY

Petersburg

VIRGINIA

Fredricktown

Raleigh

Sikeston

Nashville

NORTH CAROLINA

TENNESSEE

Charlotte

Rock Hill

SOUTH CAROLINA

Memphis

Winnsboro

ARKANSAS

Little Rock

Sumter

Birmingham

Anniston

GEORGIA

MISSISSIPPI

Shreveport

Jackson

Montgomery

LOUISIANA

McComb

ALABAMA

Tallahassee

Jacksonville

Baton Rouge

New Orleans

Ocala

Tampa

FLORIDA

→ Bus routes of the Freedom Riders

Locations where Freedom Riders encountered violence or were jailed

Freedom Riders sit on the ground after the Greyhound bus they were riding was set afire by a group of white segregationists outside Anniston, Alabama.

bus stations, the ruling was being widely ignored in the South. A northern-based civil rights organization, the Congress on Racial Equality (CORE), organized what were called Freedom Rides, a famous challenge to segregation in bus facilities.

The first Freedom Ride commenced on May 4, 1961, when seven black men, three white men, and three white women boarded a bus in Washington, D.C., for a two-week trip into the Deep South. The trip proceeded without incident until two of the black men attempted to use a white restroom in Rock Hill and were beaten by a mob of white men.

The riders decided to split up, boarding two separate buses. When one of the vehicles entered the Anniston, Alabama, bus terminal, it was surrounded by a mob of whites who smashed the windows with pipes and clubs and slashed the tires. The driver quickly pulled away from the terminal, but the tires went flat a few miles outside of town. When the mob caught up with the Freedom Rider, they set the bus on fire. The riders, choking on smoke, stumbled off the vehicle moments before the gas tanks exploded. They were beaten with baseball bats, bricks, and fists.

While the protesters were taken to the hospital, the other bus was given the same treatment in Birmingham. Riders were mercilessly beaten by Ku Klux Klansmen who used brass knuckles, lead pipes, fists, and feet. One Freedom Rider was paralyzed for life; others suffered near-fatal injuries. Police were nowhere to be found.

When Nash heard of the beatings, she was at a picnic celebrating the integration of Nashville's movie theaters. Stunned by the news, Nash virtually took over the Freedom Ride protest, organizing a group of students to ride from Nashville to New Orleans, via Birmingham and Montgomery. In the role of protest organizer, Nash had to field hundreds of phone calls from worried parents, ministers, and angry federal officials in the John F. Kennedy administration who accused the Freedom Riders of provoking the violence. When she was informed by one minister that the first Freedom Riders had been nearly killed, Nash responded: "[That's] exactly why the rides must not be stopped. If they stop us with violence, the movement is dead. We're coming."[41] Meanwhile, some of those who actually volunteered to continue the movement readied themselves for battle, as rider Lucretia Collins recalls:

I could see how strongly someone would have to be dedicated because at this point we didn't know what was going to happen. We thought that some of us would be killed. We certainly thought that some of us, if not all of us, would be severely injured. At any moment I was expecting anything. I was expecting the worst and hoping for the best.[42]

In other soldierly actions, several women made out their wills before they left Nashville. A few gave Nash sealed letters to be mailed in the event of their death. Each Freedom Rider stated, however, that she felt she must risk her life to ensure the freedom of future generations.

Not all women were frightened by the prospect, however. Some, such as eighteen-year-old Doris Ruby Smith, were energized by the fight, as Olson writes: "When [Smith] heard that Nash was recruiting students to join the Ride, she raced around Atlanta trying to raise enough money to go, too. Her appalled family and friends tried to dissuade her, but the headstrong teenager, money in hand, managed to get to Birmingham anyway."[43]

In the following days, some Freedom Riders were arrested at bus stations while others were beaten by mobs that included club-wielding white women as well as men. At a Montgomery bus station, one male Freedom Rider was held down by two men while several women and children beat his face and raked it with their fingernails. Freedom Rider Susan Wilber received similar treatment, held by men while women struck her over the head with their shoulder bags.

Protesting in Jail

While the violent racists avoided arrest, it was, ironically, the surviving Freedom Riders who were imprisoned once their buses reached Jackson, Mississippi, on June 6. One of the women, Carol Ruth Silver, had come all the way from Chicago to join the protest. In Jackson, Silver shared a 13-by-15-foot jail cell with six other white women. When she was questioned by detectives, Silver defiantly took on the role of provocateur. When asked if she had ever dated a black man, Silver replied, untruthfully, that indeed she had and she wanted to marry him.

Silver received a short hearing before a judge and was sentenced to two months in jail and a two-hundred dollar fine. She was moved to a new cell that quickly filled with Freedom Riders. Soon sixteen women were sharing a cell built to hold four prisoners.

By June 13, three cells were filled with Freedom Riders, one for whites, and two for blacks—even the jail cells were segregated at that time. Although the crowded conditions were unpleasant, the women passed the time by entertaining themselves. They exercised, played chess on a set Silver made from slices of white bread, and practiced ballet steps and folk dances. One prisoner taught the others Greek, another taught French. Silver, preparing to go to law school in the fall, even filled out her financial aid applications. With grim humor, she mailed the paperwork to the law school with the return address: Hinds County Jail, Jackson, Mississippi.

Turning Defeat into Victory

The prisoners had more to do than play chess and fill out forms, however. They continued to protest even as they were in jail voting to hold a hunger strike for male Freedom Riders who were being sent to Mississippi's notorious state penitentiary, Parchman Prison. There, the men were put in chains and forced to work picking cotton in an insulting throwback to slavery.

"Is That Sick Enough for You?"

Ruby Doris Smith, who suffered from ulcers and nausea, sometimes used unusual techniques to protest segregation. One such occasion is described in *Sisters in the Struggle* as Smith and others attempted to desegregate hospital waiting rooms at Atlanta's Grady Hospital:

Grady was a public facility that admitted both black and white patients, but it had segregated entrances and segregated areas within the hospital. Throughout late 1961 and into early 1962 Ruby Doris, along with other Atlanta students, staged a series of protests at the hospital. Movement colleague Julian Bond vividly recalls one demonstration when black students went in the hospital's white entrance. As they approached the door, the students felt butterflies in their stomachs. They knew their presence inside the white entrance would cause quite a stir, and they wondered about the reaction. They did not have to wonder long, however, because as soon as they stepped inside, the looks of surprise on the faces of white patrons quickly gave way to icy stares, and a startled white receptionist immediately told them they could not use that entrance. "And besides," she insisted in a hostile voice dripping with sarcasm, "You're not sick anyway." The woman's hostile challenge stopped the students right in their tracks like a cold slap in the face. As they milled around in confusion, Ruby Doris separated herself from the group and boldly walked up to the receptionist's desk, looked her in the eye, bent over and vomited all over the desk, straightened up and demanded to know, "Is that sick enough for you?" The receptionist's hostility quickly turned to a paralyzing confusion that rendered her speechless.

Black Freedom Rider Pauline Knight became the spokeswoman for the hunger strikers in the three cells. She demanded that the men be brought back to the city prison or that the women also be sent to Parchman. Their demand for equal treatment reflected their opposition to sexism as well as racism, as Schultz writes: "Long before the advent of widespread feminist consciousness, these women were united in their belief that they should not be treated differently than the male activists."[44]

The women soon got their wishes and were taken to Parchman, a penitentiary known for the brutality of its guards. Smith discovered this when she refused to take a shower without slippers. She was thrown in the shower by three female guards and harshly scrubbed with a floor brush.

Although the abusive treatment angered Silver and others, Smith insisted the prisoners maintain a nonviolent stance, saying, "We must not hate because that is victory for the evil forces which we are fighting. . . . [Mental] nonviolence is just as important as physical nonvio-lence . . . returning love for hate, sympathy for oppression."[45] After gaining her freedom several weeks later, Silver gave a speech commenting on the lessons she had learned from Smith:

> We were furious, we were outraged, we were seething with anger. But she, from the depth of her belief in nonviolence as a way of life . . . from her deep commitment to tenets of Christianity and the brotherhood of all mankind—it was she who ministered to our pain, it was she who urged us not to feel so badly about her beating, it was she who turned this physical defeat into a victory of love over violence and oppression.[46]

The Freedom Rides continued to bring national publicity to the racist practices of the South. After much bloodshed and controversy, public restrooms and waiting rooms were finally integrated. The women who took on the roles of protesters wore their fear, hunger, arrests, beatings, and other sufferings as badges of honor when segregation was banished forever.

Chapter 3:
Fighting for an Education

❦

Many of those who worked in the civil rights movement felt that nothing was more important than fighting for equal opportunities in education. Indeed, the performance of and conditions in African American schools in the segregated South were dismal. Nowhere was it worse than in Mississippi, which had no compulsory education law. In 1960, only 7 percent of Mississippi's black adults had finished high school compared with 42 percent of whites. The average annual education expenditure for a black pupil in Mississippi was about $22 compared with nearly $82 for every white student. In some places the disparity was even greater. For example, Holly Bluff, Mississippi, spent about $192 for every white student and only $1.25 for each black pupil. Since many children were forced by poverty to work in the fields in spring and fall, those who wanted to attend school could only do so in midsummer and winter, and meager expenditures guaranteed that the education they received on this limited basis was also the most meager. With such disparity in educational opportunities, it is hardly surprising that most African Americans were forced to work at the lowest paying jobs and live in grinding poverty, and that equal education was an extremely emotional issue in the civil rights movement.

The Citizenship School Movement

The reality of 12 million illiterate black adults in the South inspired schoolteacher Septima Clark to set up the first Citizen Schools in 1957 on tiny St. John's Island off the coast of Charleston, South Carolina. In her role as citizenship teacher, Clark opened a classroom in a few empty rooms behind a grocery store where students would not be seen by the local whites. Clark then recruited her cousin, Bernice Robinson, a beautician, to teach. Clark overrode Robinson's protests that she was a hairdresser, not a teacher:

> We don't want a certified teacher because they are accustomed to

working by a [straight-laced] curriculum. They wouldn't be able to bend, to give. We need a community worker to do it who cares for the people, who understands the people, who can communicate with the people . . . so there's nobody to do it but you. Either you do it or we don't have a school.[47]

Convinced to take on a new, unique role, Robinson worked with Clark to develop innovative teaching methods. Instead of using children's books to teach adult literacy, Robinson used money orders, driver's license exams, voter registration forms, and even the Sears department store catalog.

Evidence of the desperate need for basic literacy was sometimes poignant. For example, one woman said that someone was taking money out of her bank account because she did not know how to make out a check or examine her bank statements. As Clark writes in her autobiography *Ready from Within:*

She was in the habit of having someone white make out her check for her, and then she'd sign with an "X." So we started teaching banking. We brought in a banker and he put the whole form up on the board and showed them how to put in the date and how to write it out. He told

In a classroom with a sign on the wall pronouncing the death of Jim Crow laws, a citizenship instructor in Virginia teaches an elderly black woman to write.

them, "Don't leave a space at the end of the check. Somebody else could write another number in there."[48]

Prizing literacy for more than its value in daily activities, Clark used her classes to inspire students to become political activists. She used the Constitution as a teaching tool: "I took words out of the Constitution and divided each word into syllables and practiced pronouncing them. Then we discussed together the meaning of each word until we all understood what they meant."[49] Many of the students had never been taught that the Constitution guaranteed freedom of speech and the right of citizens to vote. As renowned voting rights advocate Fannie Lou Hamer said after attending a Mississippi Citizenship School, before that experience "I never learned anything about voting or democracy. . . . I never even heard what was in the Constitution."[50]

The first year classes were held four hours a week in January and February, the winter months when people were not needed in the fields. The classes were so popular, however, that the next year they were held for three months. Soon Citizenship Schools were established on other nearby islands and on the mainland. By 1961, thirty-seven Citizenship Schools had been established, and in the next decade nearly ten thousand people were trained as Citizenship School teachers.

As many as two hundred schools operated at one time, set up in people's kitchens, beauty parlors, and even under trees in the summertime.

Through the schools, students learned enough to register to vote. The schools, however, created not just voters but community builders who took on many roles. Some became bankers, founding credit unions. Others were caregivers who started nursing homes. Teachers set up kindergartens, and construction workers started low-income housing projects. Moreover, the schools trained a generation of civil rights activists. According to Andrew Young Jr., "The Citizenship Schools were the base on which the whole Civil Rights Movement was built."[51] Clark agreed, adding:

Citizenship Schools made people aware of the political situation in their area. We recruited the wise leaders of their communities, like Fannie Lou Hamer in Mississippi. . . . The Citizenship School classes formed the grassroots basis of new statewide political organizations in South Carolina, Georgia, and Mississippi. From one end of the South to the other, if you look at the black elected officials and the political leaders, you find people who had their first involvement in the training program of the Citizenship School.[52]

The Highlander Folk School

❧

Septima Clark developed the Citizenship Schools in conjunction with the Highlander Folk School, founded in the 1930s and located in the Tennessee mountains fifty miles northeast of Chattanooga. Historian Jacqueline A. Rouse describes Highlander in *Sisters in the Struggle:*

> Highlander sponsored workshops which concentrated on the elimination of racial stereotypes, the breaking down of social barriers, and the development of leaders. The school was attended by many black and white activists, including Rosa Parks and Martin Luther King, Jr. During the summer of 1954, following the Supreme Court's *Brown v. Board of Education* decision [banning school segregation], Clark attended the Highlander School's summer workshop. At Highlander, Clark met many whites and blacks working for an end to legal racial segregation. Workshop sessions addressed how the Supreme Court's decision could be implemented. She returned to Charleston to organize the black public school teachers. . . . In the summer of 1955, Clark carried several carloads of black Charlestonians to Highlander. Most were amazed to learn of whites who were truly interested in the plight of African Americans. They were even more dumbfounded to discover that blacks and whites actually ate, slept, and worked together at Highlander. Some of the participants from Charleston were uncertain about the full extent of the integration practiced at the school, and chose to eat from the baskets of fried chicken they brought with them. . . . By the middle of their first week, the participants had joined the others. However, such racial harmony amazed even those participants who came with organizing experience.

Despite the positive effect that Citizenship Schools had on black communities, they were considered highly controversial by most southern whites in power. Authorities soon shut down the headquarters of the Citizenship School movement at the Highlander Folk School in Monteagle, Tennessee. This did not stop the Citizenship School movement, however, and Clark took on the role of roving educator, traveling by bus to set up schools in Alabama, Georgia, South Carolina, and Tennessee. She did so even after suffering a heart attack in 1961.

Crisis in Little Rock

While Clark had to fight to educate black adults, a movement to integrate white schools and colleges was gaining momentum throughout the South. By the late summer of 1957, Little Rock, Arkansas, became a battleground when a federal court ordered the previously all-white Central High School to admit black students.

Standing seven stories high and spanning four city blocks, Central was one of the best high schools in the South. Fourteen times larger than Little Rock's African American high school, Central had science labs, an entire floor for the school band, and six departments devoted to home economics. In 1955, forty-one-year-old African American newspaper publisher Daisy Bates organized a legal campaign to integrate the school. As the case wound its way through the courts, her windows were broken by a rock-throwing mob, her house was sprayed with bullets, and a cross was burned on her lawn. A note at the base of the cross read "GO BACK TO AFRICA! KKK."[53] For Bates, however, such brutality was nothing new.

When Bates was eight years old she learned that she was adopted, and that her birth mother had been raped and murdered by a gang of white men when Bates was an infant. This knowledge fueled Bates's growing hatred for white people. As she matured, however, her adoptive father advised her to use her emotions to productive ends:

In 1957 an angry crowd of whites gathers outside Central High School in Little Rock, Arkansas, to prevent black students from entering.

Terror in Little Rock

❧

In her role as the first black student to integrate Little Rock's Central High in 1957, Elizabeth Eckford had a harrowing experience, as she recalls in John Simkin's online article "Elizabeth Eckford."

When I got in front of the school, I went up to a guard . . . [but] he just looked straight ahead and didn't move to let me pass him. . . . Just then the guards let some white students through. . . . I walked up to the guard who had let the white students in. . . . When I tried to squeeze past him, he raised his bayonet and then the other guards moved in and they raised their bayonets. They glared at me with a mean look and I was very frightened and didn't know what to do. I turned around and the crowd came toward me. They moved closer and closer. Somebody started yelling, "Lynch her! Lynch her!" . . . They came closer, shouting, "No nigger bitch is going to get in our school. Get out of here!" . . .

I sat down [at a nearby bus bench] and the mob crowded up and began shouting all over again. Someone hollered, "Drag her over to this tree! Let's take care of that nigger." Just then a white man sat down beside me, put his arm around me and patted my shoulder. He raised my chin and said, "Don't let them see you cry."

Hate can destroy you, Daisy. Don't hate white people just because they're white. If you hate, make it count for something. Hate the humiliation we are living under in the South. Hate the discrimination that eats away at the soul of every black man and woman. Hate the insults hurled at us by white scum—and try to do something about it, or your hate won't [add up to] a thing.[54]

Following this advice, Bates began publishing the *Arkansas State Press* in 1941. This weekly newspaper advocated equality for African Americans. As a civil rights crusader, Bates mounted vigorous campaigns against police brutality, slum housing, employment discrimination, and government injustice. Because of her influence, Bates was elected president of the Arkansas State Conference of NAACP branches. In this position she became the adviser to the first nine black students, known as the Little Rock Nine, who were scheduled to attend Central High.

No one could question why black students wanted to attend Central High. The all-black high school had broken tables, used books, and other damaged supplies that had been thrown away at Central. Students trying to learn under these conditions didn't so much care about civil rights. As Melba Pattillo Beals, a member of the Little Rock Nine, stated in a 1998 interview, she simply wanted to take on the role of scholar:

> We [wanted to attend] Central for opportunity. We didn't understand integration; we didn't even know the word *integration*. . . . [We] wanted to go to Central High first and foremost because of access, because of resources, because of books and good furniture. . . . It was turning out Rhodes scholars and offering the highest level of education. It was at the cutting edge in this nation. And that's what I wanted. I wanted a shot at being a Rhodes scholar. I wanted equality.[55]

That chance for equality came when a federal court ordered Arkansas officials to allow the black students into Central High on September 5, 1957. The court order, however, ignited a firestorm. Angry white mobs gathered in front of the school, yelling racial epithets and threatening violence. Orval Faubus, the governor of Arkansas and a staunch segregationist, posted the National Guard in front of the school to keep the black students out. Members of the national press were on the scene and, as Steven F. Lawson writes, one fifteen-year-old student, Elizabeth Eckford, unwittingly came to symbolize the movement:

> Eckford became the poster girl for the harrowing experience. On the

Fifteen-year-old Elizabeth Eckford braves a crowd of angry whites to become the first black student to attend Central High School.

first day of trying to attend Central, she found herself alone surrounded by a howling mob of whites attempting to deny her entry. Photographers captured her strength and courage as she remained calm and finally managed, with the help of a couple of sympathetic white bystanders, to make her way to safety.[56]

As leader of the movement to integrate Central, Bates felt responsible for the torment Eckford received. To prevent further violence, Bates attempted to walk the remaining students to the front door of the school surrounded by four ministers, two black and two white. After pushing through a mob of five hundred jeering racists, they were blocked by the National Guard. Leaving the school grounds, the group went to visit the U.S. attorney's office. He would do nothing to enforce the court order, so Bates had to direct NAACP lawyers to get a court order to prevent Faubus from using the National Guard to block the students.

The lawyers succeeded and on September 23, the students bravely tried again. Bates devised a plan to drive up to the side door of the school while the mob milled around the front door. The plan worked: the children ran to safety inside the school before the crowd noticed. As Bates sped off in her car, the mob realized what had happened. They turned their anger on black and white reporters who were covering the event. Journalists and photographers from national magazines were beaten and their cameras were destroyed. The mob screamed, cursed, and wept as the black students looked out from the school windows. Bates spent the night with shotgun-wielding friends waiting for a mob to attack her house. A stream of intimidating telephone calls, including death threats, rattled her nerves.

That evening, President Dwight D. Eisenhower ordered the 101st Airborne Division to Little Rock. In the morning, 350 paratroopers stood in front of Central High. Soldiers in jeeps mounted with machine guns took the students to school. Helicopters circled overhead. Once inside, each student was given a bodyguard. At the end of the day the students were taken home.

The students finally went to school, but Bates suffered greatly for her role in the crusade. Every day, thugs drove by her house and threw rocks and firecrackers at her windows. Her house was peppered repeatedly with shotgun blasts. When informed by a white visitor that the terrorism would stop if she called for the black students to be pulled from Central High, she steadfastly refused. Letters to the attorney general and Eisenhower did little to stop the violence.

The newspaper that Bates had run for nearly seventeen years suffered as well.

Longtime clients such as Southwestern Bell, local businesses, and the gas company refused to advertise. Bates was forced to shut down the newspaper. Nevertheless, she did not regret her part in the movement. Authors Carolyn Calloway-Thomas and Thurmon Garner describe the leadership role of Bates in their article "Daisy Bates and the Little Rock Crisis: Forging the Way":

> She created a form of organization based on centralization of information and command. For example, as early as the first day that the "Little Rock Nine" . . . were scheduled to enter school, realizing that [the school superintendent] had given the students little assurance that they would be protected from violence, Bates tackled the problem, concentrating on what should be done as well as when and how. . . . Bates demonstrated her organizational prowess in other ways as well. She orchestrated the movement of the children and their parents including when they were to arrive at her home, the route they would take to school, and even the door through which they would enter.[57]

"My Options Were Limitless"

While Bates fought to provide a decent public education for all African American children, a few thousand black students were able to attend private all-black colleges such as Fisk University in Nashville and Spelman and Morehouse in Atlanta. In the 1950s, however, most state universities were strictly segregated and barred African Americans from enrolling.

Despite the racist policies of tax-funded educational institutions, several women took on the role of civil rights pioneers and attempted to integrate state universities. The first was Autherine Lucy, from rural Alabama. Lucy grew up picking cotton, watermelons, sweet potatoes, and peanuts but went on to earn a bachelor's degree from Alabama's all-black Miles College in 1952. With her mind set on getting the best education possible, Lucy enrolled in the University of Alabama as a graduate student in library science.

After years of court battles waged by lawyers from the NAACP, Lucy arrived on the Tuscaloosa campus in February 1956. However, her car was surrounded by white students who jumped on the roof and pelted it with eggs and bricks while threatening to kill her. Riots continued for three days until campus officials suspended and then expelled Lucy, saying it was for her own protection.

Lucy's terrifying experience did not deter Charlayne Hunter-Gault from trying to desegregate the University of Georgia in 1961. Although she grew up in segregated Georgia, the young Charlayne Hunter never placed limitations on

In 1962 Charlayne Hunter-Gault became the first black woman to graduate from the University of Georgia.

strips, and her favorite character was Brenda Starr, a savvy reporter who would stop at nothing to get a good story. Although the comic-strip Starr was a white woman with red hair, Charlayne identified with the gutsy and independent character and decided she wanted to become a journalist too.

Hunter-Gault worked on her school newspaper from ninth grade until she graduated from high school in 1958. She decided that to get the best education she would have to attend the University of Georgia in Athens, which was known for its journalism program. That school was segregated, however, and Hunter-Gault was denied admission. The alleged reasons were explained in a front-page article in the *Atlanta Constitution*: "[The] university is full up . . . [and] because the dormitories are full the only freshmen [the school] can admit are those who are bona fide Athens residents."[59] Hunter-Gault knew that she was rejected for the color of her skin, not because she lived in Atlanta. She sued the university for discrimination.

After a three-year court battle, Hunter-Gault finally won the right to enroll in 1961 despite the fact that Georgia governor Ernest Vandiver vowed that "not one, no, not one"[60] black person would attend classes with whites. Meanwhile, members of the Ku Klux Klan were visiting fraternities and stirring up racist sentiments among the students.

her dreams. As she told interviewer Mary Marshall Clark in 1993: "I had been taught that my options were limitless so there was no barrier in my brain that told me to stop . . . because I wasn't supposed to go any farther."[58]

Her self-educated grandmother also served as a role model. As a child, Charlayne would sit next to her grandmother as she read the African American newspaper *Atlanta Daily World* and the mainstream papers *Atlanta Constitution* and *Atlanta Journal*. Charlayne read the comic

Women of the Civil Rights Movement

Despite the brewing trouble, Hunter-Gault sensed victory, as she writes in her autobiography *In My Place*: "I was going to take my first steps onto the campus as if I knew my place. . . . [For] the first time, it would be I who would be defining my place on my terms, on territory that was their pride but was now mine, too."[61]

White supremacists among her fellow students had other ideas, however. On the second night, Hunter-Gault was studying in her dormitory room, unaware that all the other women in the dorm had turned off the lights in their rooms. As she writes: "With the rest of the building in darkness, the three brightly lit windows of my apartment must have made an inviting target for the mob out on the lawn."[62]

A brick flew through her window, followed by a soda bottle. Soon the mob began throwing bricks and bottles through other windows, and the white women in Hunter-Gault's dorm told her to leave or become a "black martyr."[63] Although the state highway patrol headquarters was five minutes away, police did not arrive for hours. She was whisked away and later suspended, as Lucy had been, for her own safety. Viewing this action as a blatant excuse to bar her from the university, she filed suit to return to college.

Hunter-Gault was finally admitted to the University of Georgia's Henry W. Grady School of Journalism, and in 1962 became the first African American woman to graduate from the university. She went on to a celebrated career in journalism with the Public Broadcasting System and as a national correspondent for Cable News Network (CNN). Her brave stand broke down the doors of segregation, and within a few years, universities across the South were integrated. For Hunter-Gault, Eckford, and other students, the scars of racism remained. Speaking in 1998, Beals recalled the pain of living with prejudice and discrimination in Little Rock schools:

> Every single day, every moment of every day of your life when you're young, something [negative] happens. You're different. . . . Every time this happens to you, it dawns on you slowly how you're going to be living your life as a second-class citizen. . . . Nobody presents you with a handbook when you're teething, and says, "Here's how you must behave as a second-class citizen." Instead, the humiliating expectation and traditions of segregation creep over you, slowly stealing a teaspoon of your self-esteem each day. . . . It was like living in jail and I wouldn't wish it on anybody.[64]

Chapter 4:
Expanding
Voting Rights

❦

African Americans living in the South had to face the daily humiliation of Jim Crow laws that denied them the most basic rights of a democracy. While sit-ins and protests helped break down the barriers of segregation, the political landscape remained unchanged throughout the South. Almost all politicians, from small-town mayors to senators and governors, were white males. These men won elections where African Americans were denied the right to vote. And many of them held on to power with the support of white supremacists.

Pro-segregationist politicians were able to remain in power because African Americans faced many hurdles that prevented them from voting. Since the end of the Civil War, most southern states charged fees to vote, called poll taxes. In states like Mississippi where 86 percent of black people lived below the poverty level set by the federal government, poll taxes effectively kept many from voting.

There were other barriers as well. A 1954 Mississippi law required individuals registering to vote to fill out a four-page form in which they had to read and interpret the state constitution. White county registrars were empowered to grade the test. White people, no matter what their answers, always passed while black people, even those with a college education, invariably failed. Activist Winson Hudson described her two-year struggle to register in Harmony, Mississippi: "We had to fill out an application and had to read and interpret the Mississippi constitution, section 44. You had to read and interpret it to the *t*. It was little bitty writing and you had to copy it and interpret it and I mean you couldn't leave an *i* undotted."[65] In other states African American registrants were required to undergo similar types of literacy tests, sometimes up to twenty pages long. Often, even those who cleared such hurdles were further harassed or arrested on their way to the polls, and lynching was still a real threat.

Such intense pressure had been very successful in disenfranchising Mississippi's poor blacks. While the state was 45 percent black in 1960, only 5 percent of voting age blacks were registered to vote. In 1962, five counties that had black majorities did not have a single registered African American voter.

"Get Our People Organized"

Fannie Lou Hamer intended to reverse this trend in Sunflower County, where none of the county's 13,500 black adults were registered to vote. In August 1962, when she went to the county courthouse in Ruleville to register with seventeen others, she was met by an angry mob of white farmers wearing cowboy hats, carrying guns, and holding back vicious dogs.

The clerk told Hamer that she could only register if she could interpret an obscure section of the Mississippi Constitution. Hamer flunked the contrived test, and on the way back home, the bus she was riding on with the other voters was stopped for no reason. The group was temporarily jailed, and Hamer quickly experienced the most common form of punishment for registering. She was fired from her twenty-three-cents-an-hour job, as she explains: "I was fired the same day, after working on the plantation for eighteen years. My husband worked there thirty years. When my employer found out I'd been down to the courthouse [to register], she said I'd have to withdraw or be fired."[66] When Hamer returned home, her landlord told her to stop trying to register or leave the home she rented. For

An elderly black woman learns how to complete a voting ballot at a church meeting in a small Alabama town.

Food and Voting Rights

❧

In 1964, Fannie Lou Hamer played a role in charity work, distributing thousands of pounds of food and clothing collected in northern cities to impoverished African Americans in western Mississippi. Hamer insisted, however, that those receiving the charity first register to vote, as Chana Kai Lee writes in *For Freedom's Sake: The Life of Fannie Lou Hamer:*

> At times Hamer had to be blunt about drawing the link between food and voter registration, and she found it necessary to confront her neighbors and peers. On one occasion, Hamer . . . refused to give clothes and food to women who had lined up in her yard at seven o'clock in the morning to receive commodities. She chided them for being "a pack of them women [who] never even been once to [the county seat in] Indianola to try and register to help themselves!" She insisted that no one should receive assistance before one tried to help oneself. In her mind, it was only right and necessary that everyone attempt voter registration before receiving donations. Hamer reassured those women who feared losing their jobs or lives that the movement would take care of them, no matter the consequences. She told them it was important that blacks "keep pounding on that registrar's door." That morning she announced that "no food and no clothes was goin' to be distributed till all the cars come back from Indianola." She borrowed a car and, with help from other drivers, drove the women to Indianola. Hamer made sure that thirty women registered that morning.

the sake of her husband and children, Hamer left her home of eighteen years.

Aware that she had become a target of white supremacists, Hamer became a fugitive. She stayed with neighbors Robert and Mary Tucker, who were black civil rights activists. Days later, however, the Tucker house was attacked in a drive-by shooting. Although sixteen bullets pierced the walls and windows of the house, no one was hurt.

While moving from place to place for safety, Hamer studied the Mississippi Constitution with intense determination so that she could pass any test the voter registrar used to block her. On her third try at registering, in January 1963, Hamer passed the test and was duly registered to vote.

Mississippi law required that the names of registered voters be published in the legal notices section of the local newspaper for two weeks, and the appearance of Hamer's name made her the focus of an intensive hate campaign. Carloads of armed white supremacists circled the homes where she took refuge. She was showered with obscenities, threatened in anonymous phone calls, and cursed in hate mail. Hamer's response was to "work and get our people organized."[67]

Hamer joined SNCC and soon became one of the organization's leading spokespersons. She began traveling across the South working on numerous registration campaigns. On June 3, 1963, she was arrested in Winona, Mississippi, jailed, and severely beaten. Hamer described the experience:

> Three white men came into my room. One was a state highway policeman. . . . They said they were going to make me wish I was dead. They made me lay down on my face and they ordered two Negro prisoners to beat me with a blackjack. That was unbearable. The first prisoner beat me until he was exhausted, then the second Negro began to beat me. . . . They beat me until I was hard, 'til I couldn't bend my fingers or get up when they told me to. That's how I got this blood clot in my eye—the sight's nearly gone now. My kidney was injured from the blows they gave me on the back.[68]

In spite of her horrible beating, Hamer refused to back down and continued to agitate for the civil rights movement. She went on to become a force in national politics, fighting for civil rights until her death in 1977.

"A Country Diplomat"

Unlike Hamer, who worked as a poverty-stricken sharecropper most of her life, Annie Bell Robinson Devine of Caton, Mississippi, was uniquely positioned to aid the voting rights movement. Devine was an insurance agent for a black-owned company. In her daily work, she went door-to-door in Madison County, Mississippi, talking to middle-class and poor black residents. Accustomed to selling a product, Devine was at ease promoting voting rights by canvassing neighborhoods, distributing civil rights literature, and explaining the goals of the voter registration movement. In *Women in the Civil Rights Movement*, Victoria Crawford explains how Devine's job as insurance agent helped prepare her for a role as a leader of the Congress on Racial Equality (CORE) after she quit her insurance job in the early sixties:

> Like so many other grassroots organizers, Annie Devine brought a wealth of resources to the movement. Not only was she mature, level-headed, and a highly respected woman of the

community, Devine also had concrete skills that were essential to the movement's survival. From her work in insurance she had become comfortable traveling alone by car throughout the country. In addition, she had learned to work effectively with people, which was extremely useful in mass [voter] mobilization. Devine knew how to conduct meetings, and the younger CORE activists came to depend on her as an advice-giver and stabilizing force within the organization.[69]

As a middle-aged woman among the mostly young CORE members, Devine was an effective go-between, setting policy differences between rebellious college students and older male leaders, most of whom were conservative preachers. She also acted as a counselor, advising young, educated activists on effective ways to spread the message among older, unschooled citizens. As one unnamed worker said: "Mrs. Devine was a country diplomat."[70]

Volunteering for Freedom Summer

While Devine and Hamer were able to register voters in limited areas, several large civil rights organizations wanted to register as many African American voters as possible. In late 1963, SNCC and

a group called Council of Federated Organizations (COFO) planned an event called Freedom Summer. The plan for Freedom Summer was to send hundreds of SNCC workers to Mississippi in the summer of 1964, to expand black voter registration in time for the November election. There was great debate, however, over the use of white volunteers in Freedom Summer. Given the dismal state of race relations in Mississippi at the time, some did not want to work with white college students from the North. It was finally decided that white male and female workers should be used largely because their images attracted news cameras. Doug McAdam explains the rationale in *Freedom Summer*:

The fundamental goal of the project was to focus national attention on Mississippi as a means of forcing federal intervention in the state. For the project to be successful, then, it had to attract national media attention. What better way to do so than by recruiting the ... daughters of upper-middle-class white America to join the effort? Their experiences during the Freedom Vote campaign had convinced the SNCC high command that nothing attracted the media quite like scenes of white college kids helping "the downtrodden Negroes of Mississippi." The SNCC veterans had

In 1962 volunteer civil rights activists in Mississippi encourage an elderly black couple to register to vote.

also learned that the presence of well-heeled white students insured the conspicuous presence of federal law enforcement officials.[71]

The focus on image could not mask the very real risks involved in participation. SNCC workers were therefore amazed when hundreds of women volunteered for the project, and organizers had to deal with an added sexual dimension to the racial and political volatility that the white women would experience. In the Jim Crow era, white supremacists often justified violence against blacks with the unfair claim that they were protecting white women from the aggressive sexual advances of black men. Hundreds of white female college students who traveled to Mississippi for Freedom Summer in 1964 had to be prepared for attacks by white racists who would object to interracial activity of any kind. In an interview report, an SNCC staff member describes why he rejected one unnamed female volunteer whose sexually liberated attitudes might have inflamed the situation:

[The interviewer] asked her how she'd deal with a Negro man who came up to her on the street and asked to sleep with her. She said she might. I asked her what she'd do if I told her, as a staff member, that sexual activity would endanger everyone, and not to do it. She said she might go ahead and do it anyhow.[72]

A more common reason for rejecting women was that many of them refused to perform secretarial work. Despite the rejections, more than four hundred women were accepted to work for Freedom Summer, making up half of the volunteers.

Freedom High

Beginning on June 14, 1964, the eight hundred volunteers for Freedom Summer were divided into two groups for separate weeklong training sessions known as Freedom High at the Western College for Women in Oxford, Ohio. During each intense, stressful week, black southern civil rights activists attempted to turn middle-class northern college students into soldiers for the voter registration movement. This clash of cultures was a shock to relatively sheltered, idealistic, largely suburban youth. Some, such as volunteer Margaret Aley, felt that their lives were changed forever, as she confessed in a letter home to her parents: "I've never known people like [the SNCC activists] before; they are so full of heart and life. . . . They have a free-ness of spirit that I've rarely seen. . . . I feel like I've found something I've been looking for for a long time. I feel like I finally came home. I have no doubt that I belong here."[73]

While embarking on a voyage of personal discovery, volunteers were also aware that they were about to brave great danger. Each was told to prepare for death

and to carry with them at least five hundred dollars—a large sum at the time—for bail, medical emergencies, and food. They were also instructed to abandon their roles as privileged, educated Americans. One unnamed worker advised them to go to jail quietly if arrested, because "Mississippi is not the place to start conducting constitutional law classes for the policemen, many of whom don't have a fifth-grade education."[74]

The most important work of the week involved role playing, in which SNCC workers imitated the behavior of angry policemen, vicious racists, and others. In *Freedom Summer*, volunteer Sally Belfrage quotes a trainer preparing the students for a beating:

> Cover your head, roll up in a knot, hit the ground. . . . Head as close to the knees as possible. Legs together. . . . Girls, keep your skirts pinned under your knees if you're modest. Don't carry watches, pens, glasses, contact lenses, and never more than five or ten dollars. No sandals. . . . If your friend is getting his head beat, fall on him, man! What happens to one happens to everybody.[75]

Another role-playing situation involved SNCC workers yelling racist epithets and throwing stones at volunteers attempting to accompany a group of black voter registrants to a courthouse. Activists were also trained to deal with tear gas, police dogs, cattle prods, and other rough methods of crowd control.

As Belfrage writes, the volunteers were also forced, often unwillingly, to adopt the role of media stars when reporters from London to Algeria descended on the campus: "[The media] followed us into the classrooms and dormitories, around the lounges, out along the paths. They asked people to sing that [protest] song once again for the American public. There was footage, yardage, and mileage of every face in the place."[76]

"Poor, Oppressed, and Hated"

After a week of training, the first volunteers left for Mississippi, looking like both

Role Playing for Freedom Summer

When white northern college students volunteered to travel to Mississippi for Freedom Summer, they were trained as if entering a war zone. Since few northerners ever experienced the extreme racism of the 1960s South, SNCC workers engaged in role playing to familiarize the volunteers with the situation. In *Freedom Summer*, volunteer Sally Belfrage reprints a copy of an instruction sheet called "Possible Role-Playing Situations":

1. *The Cell* (four persons, white, same sex): A white civil rights worker is thrown into a cell with three ardent segregationists. As the jailer opens the cell, he identifies the civil rights worker to the inmates— "Got some company for you fellas, one of those Northern nigger-loving agitators. Now you treat him nice."

2. *Police Harassment* (seven persons, white and Negro, male and female): Two state troopers stop a carload of five civil rights workers for speeding on a little-used highway.

3. *The Guest* (seven persons, white and Negro, male and female): A white civil rights worker who is staying with a Mississippi Negro family receives an anonymous note or phone call warning him that unless [she] clears out of town by midnight the family will be attacked and the house burned to the ground.

4. *Canvassing* (five persons, white and Negro, male and female): An integrated team of civil rights workers visits a Negro home to try to persuade the adults of the family to register to vote. (Variation: While the team is talking with the family, the plantation owner arrives on the scene with a shotgun.)

"children heading for summer camp and soldiers going off to war,"[77] according to one observer. Even before the second group left, however, tragedy, struck. On June 21, 1964, three Freedom Summer volunteers—Andrew Goodman, Michael "Mickey" Schwerner, and James Chaney —disappeared in Neshoba County, Mississippi, where they had gone to investigate one in a series of church bombings. Their bodies were discovered weeks later buried in an earthen dam. All had been brutally beaten, and eventually local Klansmen, including the deputy sheriff, were held responsible for their murders.

Despite the murders of three volunteers, Freedom Summer went on as planned. Women set up Freedom Schools that taught black history, French, and adult literacy. Others became librarians, setting up places to lend books to black people for the first time. Volunteers also canvassed from sunup to sundown, walking door-to-door to register voters. This was done in a climate of such fear and violence that it caused some to get battle fatigue similar to that experienced by soldiers in combat. As Belfrage writes:

There are incipient nervous breakdowns walking around all over Greenwood [Mississippi]. . . . It has something to do with fear. Fear *can't* become a habit. But there is something extra every minute from having that minute dangerous, and if you can't convert the extra into something you have nowhere to *put* it. . . . I've got a fabulous depression, split in two—I can't bear another moment of it but it's impossible to believe that it can end in three weeks [when Freedom Summer is over]. How can I leave? How can I leave people I love so much? What made me think I could accomplish anything? . . . There's nowhere else I want to be.[78]

Belfrage's fear, depression, and anxiety were well-founded. By October, fifteen people had been murdered, four people wounded, thirty-seven black churches burned or bombed, and over one thousand arrested. In this climate of repression, many women experienced being outcasts. As one unnamed volunteer stated, "For the first time in my life, I am seeing what it is like to be poor, oppressed, and hated."[79]

Under these circumstances, older black women who had been struggling their entire lives became role models for the young women who volunteered for Freedom Summer. Many formed strong bonds as the African American women took in the volunteers and treated them like family members, feeding them, healing them when they were sick, and offering comfort and encouragement despite threats of violence. At one point a radio

"An Atmosphere of Terror"

⁂

In the summer of 1964, Michael "Mickey" Schwerner was one of three men murdered in Neshoba County, Mississippi, by local Klansmen, one of whom was a deputy sheriff. After her husband's death, Rita Schwerner, herself a civil rights activist, traveled to Philadelphia, Mississippi, hoping to aid the investigation. In May 2000, Rita Schwerner Bender spoke on the CNN show *Burden of Proof* about the conditions in Mississippi that led to her husband's death:

Mississippi was a place—as I believe most of the South was—in which an atmosphere of terror was created not just by the Klan . . . but by people in positions of power, by people in government, by people in the business community, by doctors, by lawyers, by church people, in which it was made clear that violence

was acceptable in order to continue the Jim Crow laws that existed. . . .

The state of Mississippi never brought any kind of charges in this case. . . . [You] had a series of governors who were encouraging resistance by any means. After these three men disappeared, Governor Paul Johnson, the governor of the state, joked and said they had undoubtedly gone to Cuba. . . . They created an atmosphere—the state legislature in Mississippi created a sovereignty commission, which was an arm of the state government, which was established precisely to preserve segregation and which conducted spying, which was engaged in causing people to lose their jobs, was sharing information about law-abiding citizens with members of law enforcement, who were also known to be members of the Klan.

station in Canton, Mississippi, announced a reward of four hundred dollars to anyone who would bomb a home where volunteers were staying. The fear campaign did not cause one worker to be evicted, prompting one unnamed activist to say, "Our hostesses are brave women and their fear is not at all mixed with resentment of us, but that makes it none the easier for them."[80]

A few happier moments occurred in the midst of the racial terrorism. One volunteer, Wendy Weiner, held her wedding amid the activity. Belfrage describes the scene:

Wendy put on jeans and sandals and a blue denim workshirt with the tails out, and wore her long black hair loose down her back. The chapel . . . was laden with flowers and pine twigs, and

Mississippi Freedom Summer pamphlets twined with leaves around a string that crisscrossed the low ceiling. Behind the altar . . . a SNCC poster, surrounded with more leaves and flowers, of two children sitting on a stoop with the motto: GIVE THEM A FUTURE IN MISSISSIPPI. . . . [After the ceremony, the] air was filled with rice and freedom songs; the punch, vaguely spiked with wine, was served with cookies and potato chips; the songs got faster, and outside some volunteers taught the *hora* [a traditional Jewish dance] to local teen-agers. Everybody stopped worrying for almost two hours.[81]

The Voting Rights Act

Voter registration drives similar to those in Mississippi were carried out throughout the South. And those involved experienced similar campaigns of intimidation. When Dorothy Height, president of the National Council of Negro Women (NCNW), flew into Selma for a voter registration drive, her car was followed everywhere by plainclothes policemen. When she attended a meeting at a church, the building was surrounded by hundreds of state troopers wearing yellow riot helmets decorated with the Confederate flag. These officers were armed with pistols, submachine guns, tear gas bombs, and electric cattle prods. The tear gas and clubs would later be used on men, women, and children marching for voting rights.

Height reported her Selma experience to national civil rights organizations and helped start a national movement. Groups such as the YMCA, the National Council of Jewish Women, the National Council of Catholic Women, and Church Women United began to agitate for voting rights on a national level. Through these efforts, Congress passed the Voting Rights Act in August 1965. This law empowered the federal government to oversee voter registration and elections in counties that had used prejudicial tests to determine voter eligibility or where registration or turnout had been less than 50 percent in the 1964 presidential election. For the first time in the twentieth century, African Americans were guaranteed the right to vote in every city, town, and county in the United States. The law's effects were powerful. By 1968, nearly 60 percent of eligible African Americans were registered to vote in Mississippi, and other southern states showed similar improvement. Millions of people entered the voting booth for the first time thanks to Hamer, Height, and thousands of lesser-known men and women who faced beatings and risked their lives to guarantee their right to vote.

Chapter 5: Women in Political Office

Many of the most important victories in the civil rights movement have taken place in the voting booth. Before the Voting Rights Act was signed by President Lyndon Johnson in 1965, only about 470 black elected officials served in local and national political office in the United States. Forty years later, the number of African Americans holding elective office in the United States has jumped to over 9,000, about 3,200 of whom are black women. As Linda Faye Williams writes in *Sisters in the Struggle*, this has been one of the most positive aspects of the civil rights movement in the past fifty years: "While . . . [economic] indicators such as the median income and the poverty rate demonstrate only murky progress at best in altering the relative condition of the black population . . . the election of blacks to public office, largely as a result of the Voting Rights Act, demonstrates one straight line of upward growth."[82]

Political Candidate

Even before the Voting Rights Act was passed, civil rights activists such as Fannie Lou Hamer recognized the need for African American women to take on the roles of politicians. Hamer believed that the stranglehold that racist politicians had on Mississippi could only be broken if African Americans could rely on political representation in national office. In early 1964, Hamer had been a registered voter for only two years, and she had no experience in politics. However, she became the first black woman to run for Congress from Mississippi's Second Congressional District.

Soon after Hamer announced her candidacy, intense harassment began. A telephone operator questioned why she was making so many calls, why her bill was so high, why she called someone in Texas, and why she had let outsiders use her telephone. When Hamer reminded the operator that her bill was paid and her calls were none of the operator's business, the operator warned Hamer against speaking to out-of-state civil rights activists. Hamer also received numerous death threats, about which the feisty

Fannie Lou Hamer, seen here addressing a crowd in Washington, D.C., founded a political party in Mississippi to challenge white candidates running for office.

Hamer replied: "I've been in hell for 46 years; it doesn't make any difference. . . . [I'm fully prepared] to fall five feet four inches forward in the fight for freedom."[83]

Hamer campaigned for office as both an orator and door-to-door saleswoman. With little money for bumper stickers or advertising, she relied on inspirational speeches at large rallies and simply knocking on doors in her district to ask people for their vote. Hamer's bid failed, however, when she lost the Democratic primary to the influential white male congressman Jamie Whitten, who had held the seat since 1941.

"I Question America"

Undeterred by her loss, Hamer took on the task of founding a new political party, the Mississippi Freedom Democratic Party (MFDP), to challenge the all-white roster of candidates from the state. The party held a primary and selected three black women, Hamer, Annie Devine, and Victoria Gray, to run for seats in Congress.

Creating a political party to compete with the all-white Democratic Party, which at that time controlled most political offices in the South, was a daunting undertaking. To form a new party, the women were required to organize executive committees that would oversee precinct meetings and political conventions at county and state levels. The statewide convention in Jackson, Mississippi, was attended by eight hundred men and women on August 6, 1964. Sixty-eight people, including Hamer, Devine, and Gray, were elected as delegates to attend the 1964 Democratic National Convention in Atlantic City, New Jersey.

Hamer, Devine, Gray, and the other delegates were not recognized by the national Democratic leadership, however. As a compromise, the MFDP was offered two nonvoting seats on the delegation, an offer the MFDP rejected. Stung by the defeat, Hamer mesmerized the nation on August 26, when she gave a televised eight-minute speech where she spoke of the violent beating she had received in 1962 when she tried to register to vote in Winona, Mississippi. She concluded with these words: "If the Freedom Democratic Party is not seated now I question America. Is this America, the land of the free and the home of the brave, where we have to sleep with our telephones off of the hook because our lives be threatened daily, because we want to live as decent human beings in America?"[84]

Hoping to deflect attention from Hamer's eloquent testimony, President Lyndon Johnson called a hastily scheduled speech of his own, but it was too late. The television networks covered her story, and a national audience was exposed to the brutality faced by African Americans trying to vote in the South.

The Freedom Vote

Although the Mississippi Freedom Democratic Party did not accomplish its goals at the convention, Hamer and Devine attempted to run for Congress in November 1964. Their candidacy as members of the MFDP was rejected by the Mississippi State Elections Commission because

The Faith Connection

African American women politicians often relied on biblical principles during the civil rights era. Fannie Lou Hamer, for example, often cited the Bible in speeches stating that, in her belief, God was not pleased with the way black people were brutalized and murdered in Mississippi. In *Sisters in the Struggle*, Victoria Gray, who founded the Mississippi Freedom Democratic Party with Hamer, speaks of what she calls her "faith connection" in relation to her political beliefs:

It doesn't matter what area I am in, my faith connection is my mainstay. My faith connection has been with me in all that I've ever done, whether it was in the community at large, whether it was in the political arena. I came to appreciate the importance of people being involved in the political arena. I think people who are involved in the political arena who do not have a spiritual base are the people who want to build bigger and bigger jails, spend more and more on defense, and get people off of welfare onto workfare, but they don't have any jobs for them to work on. The lack of a spiritual base on which one functions is just so destructive as opposed to those who have one.

Hamer and Devine had run in the regular Democratic primary and lost. The women then sought to get on the ballot as independent candidates and gathered enough signatures on petitions to do so. The Elections Commission, however, denied that the women had the proper amount of signatures. (It was later discovered that many valid petitions were thrown into the trash by election officials.)

With opposition at every turn, the women combined creativity and hard work to do something unique in American history: hold a nationwide mock election during the November presidential election. It was called the "Freedom Vote."

Annie Devine, Fannie Lou Hamer, and Victoria Grey (left to right) were barred from running for Congress in 1965.

The women oversaw the installation of polling booths in black churches, schools, and community centers throughout the state. The candidates gained experience in the political process as well, according to one unnamed worker, "from organizing rallies to writing speeches, from debating political issues to using sound trucks, plastering the community with posters and bumper strips [stickers]."[85]

The results were encouraging: The women won their election by huge margins. Devine beat Democrat Arthur Winstead 6,000 votes to 4. Hamer triumphed over Whitten 33,009 to 59. Although the results were not valid, in *For Freedom's Sake: The Life of Fannie Lou Hamer*, Chana Kai Lee explains the reasoning behind the Freedom Vote: "The mock election proved overwhelmingly that white politicians were ignoring the voices of Mississippi's eligible black electorate by not giving them a chance to register. Mississippi politicians had argued that low black registration figures were the result of apathy and ignorance."[86]

Armed with winning numbers, the MFDP candidates mounted what was called the "congressional challenge." When the U.S. Congress convened in January 1965, the MFDP sought to prevent the Democratic winners from being seated, arguing that the white congressmen had been illegally elected, since black voters were largely prevented from voting. With over fifteen thousand pages of sworn testimony that documented the harassment, terrorism, and violence directed against African Americans who tried to register and vote, the party hoped to prove that the discriminatory voting practices violated the constitutional rights of African Americans.

Devine, Gray, and Hamer were chosen to represent the MFDP in the congressional challenge. All three were middle-aged mothers with responsibilities to their children and households. In their commitment to political activism, however, they took on the roles of lobbyists, moving to Washington, D.C., to unseat the state's five congressmen. The women also organized support groups for people to call their representatives and ask them to challenge the seating of the congressmen.

The case wound its way through congressional committees for the next eight months. When the vote was finally taken on September 15, it was apparent that the women would lose their challenge on a series of legal and procedural technicalities. However, John W. McCormack, the sympathetic Speaker of the House, allowed the women to take seats on the House floor while the vote was taken. As a result, Hamer, Gray, and Devine were the first black women to sit on the floor of Congress. The gesture did little to satisfy the women, however, and Gray stated: "Until the time comes, that they

[House members] are ready to argue the Constitution instead of technicalities, the Constitution will not be real to me or to hundreds of thousands of other people."[87]

Although the women were once again defeated and disillusioned, their congressional challenge had a lasting effect. Their compelling testimony and reams of documents generated support for the Voting Rights Act that was passed later in the year. After passage of the act, more than a quarter million African Americans registered to vote in Mississippi, and federal registrars oversaw elections in the state and elsewhere in the South. Addressing the issue of black women's roles in this success, Victoria Crawford writes in *Sisters in the Struggle:*

[The] leadership and activism of African American women [were] central to the cultivation of [home-grown] leadership and the significant changes in Mississippi society. The systematic use of violence and terrorism and the legacy of black exclusion were formidable forces to overcome, yet black women were pivotal in mobilizing and sustaining the movement in local communities throughout the state. Perhaps their effective roles as agents of social change derived from . . . their experiences with race, gender, and class. Fannie Lou Hamer, Annie Devine, and Victoria Gray had long histories as community and church workers before they entered the political sphere. Their skills and leadership abilities positioned them at the center of local community networks, which was essential to the movement's success.[88]

The work of the MFDP opened doors for black candidates within the Democratic Party, and in 1968 most southern states sent biracial delegations to the national convention in Chicago. By 1972, the effects of Devine, Gray, and Hamer's efforts were even more impressive. Mississippi's delegation to the Democratic National Convention was 56 percent African American, and many of the black delegates were women. This caused one older, unnamed white delegate to say: "I never thought I'd see the day that middle-aged white males would be our biggest minority."[89]

"Unbought and Unbossed"

Although the efforts of the MFDP made history, the first black woman in Congress was not from the South but from New York City. In 1968, when Adam Clayton Powell Jr. was the only African American member of Congress, Shirley Chisholm broke the race and gender barrier to represent New York's Twelfth Congressional District. Like other black women in politics, Chisholm played many roles before being elected to Congress.

When Chisholm first entered politics in the 1950s, she was a volunteer for the Democratic club in her Lower East Side district. Men in the club held very powerful jobs, choosing candidates for mayor, city council, and state assembly. However, like other women in the club, Chisholm was assigned the duties of organizing food and decorations for fund-raisers, ringing doorbells to solicit donations, stuffing envelopes with campaign material, and driving voters in car pools on election day. In 1961, unhappy with these roles, Chisholm formed her own organization, the Unity Democratic Club. The goal of the club was to register black and Latino voters in Chisholm's district. In her autobiography *Unbought and Unbossed*, Chisholm listed other work of the club: "Our platform stressed integration, better schools, higher wages, more jobs, better health care, housing and transportation, more lighting, sanitation . . . youth services for the neighborhood, and full representation for black and Puerto Rican citizens."[90]

Chisholm's platform was widely appreciated in her district and made her a well-known political operative. In 1963 she capitalized on her popularity by running for the office of state assemblywoman and won the election by a landslide. In her new role, Chisholm sponsored civil rights legislation such as the bill that funded a program called SEEK, or Search for Education, Elevation, and Knowledge.

The SEEK bill provided college scholarships to minority youth.

In 1968, the forty-four-year-old Chisholm had to fight sexism again

The Role of Women in Politics

African American women running for political office have to fight the twin prejudices of racism and sexism. However, as Congresswoman Shirley Chisholm writes in her 1970 autobiography *Unbought and Unbossed,* women have long played extremely important roles in politics:

Men always underestimate women. They underestimated me, and they underestimated the women like me. If they had thought about it, they would have realized that many of the homes in black neighborhoods are headed by women. They stay put, raise their families—and register to vote in greater numbers. The women are always organizing for something, even if it is only a bridge club. They run the PTA, they are the backbone of the social groups and civic clubs, more than the men. . . .

Discrimination against women in politics is particularly unjust, because no political organization I have seen could function without women. They do the work that the men won't do. I know,

because I have done it all. For years I stayed in the wings and worked to put men in office, even writing their speeches and cueing them on how to answer questions. They would still be exploiting my abilities if I had not rebelled.

In 1969 Shirley Chisholm became the first black woman to be elected to Congress. She ran for president in 1972.

when she decided to run for Congress. According to Chisholm, her Republican opponent, James Farmer, "toured the district with sound trucks manned by young dudes with [full, curly hairdos called] Afros, beating on tom-toms; the big, black, male image. He drew television cameras like flies. . . . The television stations ignored the little female who was running against him."[91] While Farmer paid for this spectacle with financial backing from the national Republican Party, Chisholm had to run her campaign with little money, relying on research and creativity to get voters' attention. Having done the work of registering voters in her district, Chisholm was aware that women outnumbered men by a margin of more than two to one. Taking advantage of this information, Chisholm had shopping bags printed with her campaign slogan "Fighting Shirley Chisholm —Unbought and Unbossed."[92] Campaign workers at housing projects, markets, clinics, and subway stops handed out these bags filled with campaign literature. Female voters in this district understood that the bags were useful to maids and other laborers who used them to carry their clothes and lunches back and forth to work. By appealing to women's needs, Chisholm won the election, earning twice as many votes as her opponent.

When she went to Washington, D.C., in January 1969, the first black woman in Congress joined only 8 other African Americans and 8 other women in the 415-member House of Representatives. In Chisholm's opinion, options for change were limited by the composition and background of the congressmen:

[Our] troubled, embattled, urban society, looking to Washington for wisdom and help, finds that the processes of change are thwarted by the control of old men whose values are those of a small-town lawyer or a feed-store operator. If they react at all to the challenge of our age, it is with incomprehension and irritation. Congress seems drugged and inert most of the time. Even when the problems it ignores build up to crises and erupt in strikes, riots, and demonstrations, it is not moved.[93]

Chisholm reacted to this inertia by taking on the role of legislator for the poor. She sponsored bills that provided student loans and scholarships to minorities, older students, and women. During this era when the United States was fighting in Vietnam, Chisholm also felt that the war was immoral and that the military draft was racist, since black soldiers far outnumbered whites. She urged money to be cut from the defense budget and introduced legislation to end the draft.

In 1972, Chisholm took on another

role—that of presidential candidate—when she became the first black woman to run for president. Although she did not think she could win, Chisholm campaigned across the country. In speech after speech, she told national audiences of the discrimination that minorities and women often encountered. Although she was not elected, Chisholm continued in her role as congresswoman until 1982.

Prejudice Against Women

In the years before the women's equality movement, Congresswoman Shirley Chisholm believed women had to endure prejudice—in the form of sexism—similar to the racism faced by African Americans. Chisholm compared racism and sexism in an address she gave to the House of Representatives on May 21, 1969:

[When] a young woman graduates from college and starts looking for a job, she is likely to have a frustrating and even demeaning experience ahead of her. If she walks into an office for an interview, the first question she will be asked is, "Do you type?"

There is a calculated system of prejudice that lies unspoken behind that question. Why is it acceptable for women to be secretaries, librarians, and teachers, but totally unacceptable for them to be managers, administrators, doctors, lawyers, and Members of Congress?

The unspoken assumption is that women are different. They do not have executive ability, orderly minds, stability, leadership skills, and they are too emotional.

It has been observed before, that society for a long time, discriminated against another minority, the blacks, on the same basis—that they were different and inferior. . . . As a black person, I am no stranger to race prejudice. But the truth is that in the political world I have been far oftener discriminated against because I am a woman than because I am black.

Prejudice against blacks is becoming unacceptable. . . . Prejudice against women is still acceptable. There is very little understanding yet of the immorality involved in double pay scales and the classification of most of the better jobs as "for men only."

Making Good Law

As Chisholm broke down racial and gender barriers in New York, Barbara Jordan was pioneering new roles for black women in Texas. In 1959, after she graduated from law school, she was one of the few black female lawyers in Texas. Jordan's law practice led her into politics, and in 1966 she was elected to the Texas state senate, beating her white opponent two to one. With this victory, the thirty-year-old Jordan became the first female African American state senator in Texas and the first black person to serve in the state senate since 1883.

More than 450 African Americans showed up at the state capital on January 7, 1967, to cheer and applaud as Jordan arrived for her first day in the senate. However, the senate chamber was not ready for Jordan, since it did not have a women's restroom. The state was forced to remodel one of the committee rooms for use as a women's lounge. Senators derisively called it the "Barbara Jordan Memorial Bathroom,"[94] but this was

Congresswoman Barbara Jordan, pictured here with Jimmy Carter at the 1976 Democratic National Convention, dedicated her career to helping the disenfranchised.

hardly Jordan's only problem. Many of the segregationists in the senate resented having to deal with a black woman as an equal. Senator Dorsey Hardeman, for example, openly stated that he "wasn't going to let no nigger woman tell him what to do."[95]

Jordan refused to be intimidated or drawn into a confrontation by the blatant racism. Instead she built relationships, learned the rules of the senate, and made inroads with even the most resistant senators. Although the liberal members of the senate questioned her concessions to hardened racists, Jordan explained her reasoning:

> They held the power with their seniority and conservatism. I knew it would be well if I could work my way to them, if they could see me as a legitimate member of the Senate. I don't mean bowing and scraping and shining their shoes. I mean doing my work on the committees, asking the right kinds of questions that make good law. I wanted them to respect me for my ability as a member of that body.[96]

As state senator, Jordan worked to improve civil rights for the poor. She worked on a bill that would raise the pay of farmworkers who were mostly black and Hispanic, and she defeated sales tax bills that she said would hurt poor people. Her work gained her national attention, and when she decided to run for the United States Congress in 1972, Jordan was the most famous woman in Texas. She easily won the seat representing Houston's Fifth Ward and, in doing so, became the first black woman from the South to ever serve in Congress. On the advice of former president Johnson, Jordan requested and received a seat on the House Judiciary Committee.

A year after Jordan's historic election, Republican president Richard Nixon came under investigation for his role in the Watergate scandal when his aides were caught breaking into the Democratic Party headquarters. In her new role on the Judiciary Committee, Jordan was faced with the serious task of deciding whether or not to recommend impeachment for Nixon. While her focus in politics had always been the rights of the hardworking black people in her district, she felt a grave new responsibility toward the Constitution that only recently had been used to provide equal rights to African Americans. In her role as judge of the president, she voiced her faith in the Constitution in June 1974 when Congress was deciding Nixon's fate:

> Earlier today we heard the beginning of the Preamble to the Constitution of the United States, "We, the People." It is a very eloquent beginning.

But when that document was completed on the 17th of September in 1787, I was not included in that "We, the people." I felt somehow for many years that George Washington and Alexander Hamilton must have left me out by mistake. But through the process of amendment, interpretation, and court decision I have finally been included in "We, the People."

Today, I am an inquisitor . . . [and nothing could] overstate the solemnness that I feel right now. My faith in the Constitution is whole, it is complete, it is total. I am not going to sit here and be an idle spectator to the diminution, the subversion, the destruction of the Constitution [by Richard M. Nixon].[97]

Jordan and the majority of the Judiciary Committee voted to impeach the president. Before the full Congress could take up the matter, Nixon became the first president in U.S. history to resign. With this crisis over, Jordan continued to put in fourteen- to sixteen-hour days working to help disenfranchised people. Among her proudest accomplishments was the Voting Rights Act of 1975. This bill strengthened the Voting Rights Act of 1965 to represent Native Americans and Mexican Americans, many of whom were prevented from voting in the Southwest because they did not speak English.

In 1976, a Gallup poll named Jordan the fourth most admired woman in the United States. Riding a wave of popularity, she took on the role as national spokeswoman for the Democratic Party. In August 1976 she became the first woman as well as the first African American to give a keynote speech at a Democratic National Convention. When she spoke to a cheering crowd, she started with these words:

> It was 144 years ago that members of the Democratic Party first met in convention to select their presidential candidate. . . . It would have been most unusual for any national political party to have asked a Barbara Jordan to make a keynote address. . . . Most unusual. But tonight I am here. . . . [My] presence is one additional bit of evidence that the American Dream need not be forever deferred.[98]

In her roles as orator, lawyer, presidential inquisitor, and congresswoman, Jordan spoke for millions of people, both black and white, male and female. Along with other African American women who fought for political equality, she represented not only herself but also the American dream to all those who cared to embrace it.

Chapter 6:
Radicals and Militants

By the mid-1960s, protests, sit-ins, and battles for school integration had netted many legal gains for African Americans. A decade of favorable Supreme Court rulings and passage of the Civil Rights and the Voting Rights acts legally enshrined equality in employment, public accommodations, and the right to vote for all African Americans. While many praised these advances, the new laws passed by Congress did little to change the racism, poverty, and injustice people continued to experience in their day-to-day lives. Many activists were increasingly angry, impatient with the pace of progress, and disillusioned with the nonviolent philosophy of the civil rights movement. In 1966, these feelings ignited the Black Power movement that quickly spread across the United States.

The term Black Power was coined by SNCC chairman Stokely Carmichael after his arrest at a civil rights rally in Greenwood, Mississippi. After he was bailed out of jail, Carmichael gave a speech to a large crowd that had gathered around the courthouse. As his voice rose above the crowd, he said, "I ain't going to jail no more.... What we gonna start saying now . . . is black power."[99] Suddenly the crowd began chanting "Black Power! Black Power!" and a new movement was born. According to an SNCC policy statement of that time, "[Black Power] is a call for black people in this country to unite, to recognize their heritage, to build a sense of community. It is a call for black people to begin to define their own goals, to lead their own organizations, and to support those organizations."[100]

Sex and Separatism

Carmichael was committed to black separatism, and SNCC soon began to expel its white staff members, most of whom were women who had stayed on with the organization after Freedom Summer in 1964. While devotion to the concept of Black Power was the ostensible reason for purging SNCC of whites, other factors were involved. As SNCC worker Dion Diamond recalls:

In 1966 Stokely Carmichael addresses a crowd in Berkeley, California, calling for a new era of Black Power and black separatism.

[Male civil] rights workers were . . . somewhat analogous to a present-day jock, or a movie star, or a player [in] a big band. And there were groupies. I mean it was instant access to, at least for the men, sex. Unabated sex. And I think if there were one hundred . . . black civil rights workers, I would dare say that 99 percent took advantage of it.[101]

Such sexual politics created tension between white and black women. White women involved in romantic relationships with black SNCC workers were seen as usurping the political power of some black women within the organization. At the same time, as Evans writes, black women were questioning their sexual roles and developing their own standards of beauty: "Deeply resentful of the attraction of white women to black men, [black women] began to search for definitions of femininity that included blackness. [SNCC leader Doris Ruby Smith] herself hated white women for a period of years when she realized that they represented a cultural ideal of 'beauty and femininity.'"[102]

Whatever Smith's feelings about white women, SNCC took a more radical turn when she was elected executive secretary of the organization in 1966. Observers could not help but notice that Smith had an aggressive new vision for SNCC when, during an election meeting, she picked up a pistol and went outside to practice sharpshooting. Although she had a smile on her face, her belligerent attitude disturbed some older SNCC members who had argued against ejecting white members.

Black Male Dominance

Smith and other black women within SNCC supported Black Power. However, according to Cynthia Griggs Fleming in *Soon We Will Not Cry*, the new movement was based on the belief in black male dominance. For so long . . . black men had been virtually emasculated by white American society. Thus, [men] must assume leadership roles and reclaim their masculinity as a prerequisite to

Sexual Politics

African American women in the Black Power movement fought both for racial equality and for freedom from white standards of female beauty. In a July 1970 issue of the newspaper the *Militant*, Maxine Williams, a member of the New York City Young Socialist Alliance, discusses these sexual stereotypes:

As if Black women did not have enough to contend with . . . she also finds herself fighting the beauty "standards" of a white western society.

Years ago it was a common sight to see Black women wearing blond wigs and rouge, the object being to get as close to the white beauty standard as one possibly could. But, in spite of the fact that bleaching creams and hair straighteners were used, the trick just didn't work. . . . She was constantly being compared to the white woman, and she was the antithesis of what was considered beautiful. Usually when she saw a Black man with a white woman, the image she had of herself became even more painful.

But now, "Black is beautiful," and the Black woman is playing a more prominent role in the movement. But there is a catch! She is still being told to step back and let the Black man come forward and lead. . . .

So today, the Black woman still finds herself up the creek. She feels that she must take the nod from "her man," because if she "acts up" then she just might lose him to a white woman. She must still subordinate herself, her own feelings and desires, especially when it comes to the right of having control of her own body.

the empowerment of all black people. Some reasoned that men could only assume their rightful place if women would step aside and stop interfering.[103]

Yet Smith and the many other female members of the organization were able to assume leadership roles, despite appearances that SNCC was run by men. As SNCC member Joyce Ladner writes:

None of these [SNCC] women knew they were oppressed because of their gender. No one had ever told them that. They had grown up in a culture where they had the opportunity to use all of their skills and all of their talents to fight racial and class oppression— more radically than anything else. They took their sexuality for granted, for it was not as problematic to them as their race and their poverty.[104]

Despite their positions as strong female SNCC leaders, women continued to struggle with gender roles in the Black Power movement. As SNCC leader and Marxist intellectual Angela Davis wrote about her experiences in the civil rights movement in 1968:

I ran headlong into a situation which was to become a constant problem in my political life. I was criticized very heavily, especially by male members . . . for doing a "man's job." Women should not play leadership roles, they insisted. A woman has to "inspire" her man and educate his children. . . . Some of the brothers came around only for staff meetings . . . and whenever we women were involved in something important, they began to talk about "women taking over the organization." . . . All the myths about black women surfaced. (We) were too domineering; we were trying to control everything, including the men—which meant by extension that we wanted to rob them of their manhood. By playing such a leadership role in the organization, some of them insisted, we were aiding and abetting the [white] enemy, who wanted to see black men weak and unable to hold their own.[105]

Cool, Intellectual Duchess

While fighting sexism and racism, Davis was dedicated to Black Power. Early in 1968 she was instrumental in forming a Los Angeles offshoot of SNCC called LA SNCC. Working for the organization, Davis became an energetic activist, organizing rallies to protest police brutality and raising money in urban neighborhoods to defend black leaders on charges ranging from drug possession to murder. Davis also organized youth programs such as the SNCC Youth Corp and the Liberation School to teach black history and culture as well as revolutionary political philosophy. During this period, the FBI, the CIA, and other government agencies began watching Davis's actions very closely. The attention from authorities, however, did not stop Davis but rather made her a national media star. As her poster began to appear on the walls of meeting rooms and college dormitories, Davis was elevated to the status of a revolutionary icon among white middle-class Americans.

Davis's transformation during this period from a shy college student to an outspoken revolutionary was detailed in the *New York Post* by Helen Dudar, who wrote: "The cool intellectual with the carriage of a duchess, the detached onlooker, became a full participant—a rangy, chain-smoking black woman with a glorious Afro [hairstyle] who ran with the Panthers and signed up with the Communists."[106]

Although she was among the most well-known black female civil rights leaders, Davis, ironically, spent much of

Radical Black Power activist Angela Davis speaks at a 1974 rally in Raleigh, North Carolina. Davis opposed police brutality and worked tirelessly for civil rights.

her time as a secretary in the busy SNCC offices, fielding telephone reports of discrimination and police brutality. Davis's work with LA SNCC soon ended, however. She had maintained an excellent academic record in the course of her radical political activism, and accepted a faculty position as an assistant professor of philosophy at UCLA. The controversies surrounding Davis made her a celebrity on campus; when she appeared for her first class she was greeted by a cheering crowd of two thousand. Although she was a popular teacher, Davis continued her political activism within the black community, taking on the often thankless role of fighting for the rights of black prisoners in early 1970.

Davis's work was interrupted when several guns that belonged to her were used by a murderer who killed a judge at a courthouse in Marin County, California. Davis was charged with first degree murder for allegedly having purchased three of the four guns used in the commission of the crime. Feeling as if she would never receive a fair trial, Davis became an outlaw when she was added to the FBI's "Ten Most Wanted" fugitive list.

Davis managed to elude the FBI for two months before she was arrested in October 1970. Fearing that she was a flight risk, authorities held Davis in prison without bail for sixteen months, much of that time in solitary confinement. The publicity of her case inspired the international "Free Angela Davis" campaign. In 1972 a jury acquitted her of all charges. When her ordeal was over, Davis cofounded the National Alliance Against Racism and Political Repression, which continues its work in the civil rights and prisoner's rights movement.

"A Tool of the Revolution"

Davis was only the most visible of hundreds, perhaps thousands, of black female revolutionaries. Many belonged to the Black Panther Party (BPP), founded in Oakland in 1966 by Huey Newton and Bobby Seale. The goal of the organization was to recruit angry, alienated young black men to teach them armed self-defense against hostile inner-city police forces. For obvious reasons, law enforcement officials considered the Black Panthers a threat, and almost from the beginning, members and supporters were tracked by the FBI and aggressively targeted by police forces.

The Panthers had more on their agenda than violent confrontation with authorities, however. The organization instituted social programs that were extremely helpful to children and single mothers. As a hybrid civil rights organization that combined revolutionary philosophy with more moderate outreach programs, the Panthers organized community services such as free breakfasts for

Vanguard of the Revolution

Black Panther leaders inspired some African American women to take on the role of revolutionary. A speech by a Panther known as Bunchy Carter, published in *A Taste of Power* by former Black Panther Elaine Brown, is an example of the inflammatory antiauthoritarian rhetoric common in 1967:

I also came here to let you know that it is the position of the Black Panther Party for Self Defense that we are the vanguard of revolution in the United States. We are the vanguard party. And the vanguard party is declaring all-out-war on the pig [white policemen]. We are declaring war, and we are declaring that from this point forward, nobody will speak about Black Power or revolution unless he's willing to follow the example of the vanguard, willing to pick up the gun, ready to die for the people. . . .

[We] must deal with the pig if we are to call ourselves men. We can no longer allow the pig's armed forces to come into our communities and kill our young men and disrespect our Sisters and rob us of our lives. The pig can no longer attack and suppress our people, or send his occupying army to maraud and maim our communities, without suffering grave consequences.

From this point forward, Brothers and Sisters, if the pig moves on this community, the Black Panther Party will deal with him. . . . We're here to say that the vanguard party will deal with the pig. We'll kill the pig! . . . We will destroy him absolutely and completely or, in the process, destroy the gravitational pull between the earth and the moon!

Bobby Seale (left) and Huey Newton founded the militant Black Panther Party in 1966.

Radicals and Militants

children and free health clinics. They taught black history and revolutionary doctrine to grade schoolers while giving away free clothing to mothers. Panthers led rent strikes that allowed some tenants to buy their apartment buildings and held campaigns to gain community oversight of police departments. By performing such neighborhood-oriented tasks, the BPP became quite popular with women —by 1969 there were Black Panther chapters in thirty-seven cities and many recruits were female.

While grassroots leaders provided for their communities, top Black Panther leaders preached violent revolution and used military discipline to maintain loyalty. In *A Taste of Power*, Elaine Brown describes the radical roles women were expected to play in the Black Panther Party in 1967, according to a Panther named Ericka Huggins:

> As women, our role was not very different from that of the men, except in certain particulars. Ericka told us point-blank that as women we might have to have a sexual encounter with "the enemy" at night and slit his throat in the morning—at which we all groaned. She reminded us of the Vietnamese guerrilla women, who were not only carrying guns but using their very bodies against the American forces.... Our gender was but another weapon, another tool of the revolution. We also had the task of producing children, progeny of revolution who would carry the flame when we fell, knowing that generations after us would prevail. No matter how impossible our objective, she went on in the softest manner, the revolution would be won.[107]

The twenty-five-year-old Brown was ordered to sell the *Black Panther* newspaper every day on street corners. She was also instructed to remain on call twenty-four hours a day in case she was needed by Panther leaders for any reason. Women were advised to read and memorize the words in *Red Book* by Chinese Communist leader Mao Zedong so that they could recite portions of the book on command.

"My Rage Was So Intense"

In addition to selling papers and memorizing political dogma, Brown was expected to take on dangerous missions. She was often assigned to ride with men who were transporting caches of rifles, shotguns, and ammunition that were hidden under baby blankets. Brown's role in this mission was to act as decoy, as it was believed that police would be less likely to stop a car with a well-dressed woman in it. Although she faced arrest and possible death, she also had to fend off advances from the men. A Panther known as Franco, for example, wanted Brown to accompany him on a patrol, telling her: "Sister you're so beautiful, I'd like you to ride with me tonight. . . . When you ride with me, I'll take out two pigs just for you. Would you like me to do that for you?"[108]

Although Brown rejected Franco's advances, she was soon involved with Newton, one of the leading black revolutionaries of the 1960s. Newton appointed Brown to write and edit the *Black Panther* newspaper. This job required her to stay up for days, writing, rewriting, and editing the paper. In this job, Brown was tormented by Panther leader Bobby Seale, who often arrived at the newspaper office, criticized her work, and ordered last-minute changes. Brown describes the severe abuse she suffered when she was an hour late with the newspaper one morning:

Bobby began screaming at me. It would cost the party money. . . . Too much time had been spent editing, he shouted, looking at me. I was the editor, and I was responsible, and I was subject to discipline for that. I took the punishment the way most comrades did. Bobby's order was sufficient. There was no real appeal. . . . So I silently faced the punishment, which was always an act of violence. [Bobby's brother] John Seale was strangely gentle with the ten lashes I received from

the whip he held. We were in a small basement room at national headquarters. My bare back hardly felt the sting. . . . My rage was so intense, each lash stung me only with the face of Bobby, who was not there. My skin developed welts but was unbroken by the tenth lash. I refused the attempts of John and the other men there to put salve on my back.[109]

The harsh treatment only cemented Brown's desire to take more control of the Panthers. She was given the chance to become the first female leader of the Black Panthers in 1974 after Newton, charged with murder, turned power over to her before fleeing the United States. Brown led the Panthers until 1977. During her ten years in the organization, she was an editor, writer, revolutionary, abuse victim, and leader. In the end, she felt that she was primarily an adversary of black men, writing:

A woman in the Black Power movement was considered, at best, irrelevant. A woman asserting herself was a pariah. A woman attempting the role of leadership was, to my proud black Brothers, making an alliance with the "counter-revolutionary, man-hating, lesbian, feminist white bitches." It was a violation of some Black Power principle that was left undefined. If a black woman assumed

Elaine Brown (left), pictured here at a 1971 press conference with Huey Newton (second from left), become the first female leader of the Black Panthers.

a role of leadership, she was said to be eroding black manhood, to be hindering the progress of the black race. She was an enemy of black people.[110]

"Declaration of War"

Brown's struggle with her role in the Black Panthers was largely unknown to outsiders. The tactics and tenets of the organization, however, inspired a few young white women who believed that they could permanently change society with aggressive tactics. This led to the creation of a radical fringe group known as the Weathermen or Weather Underground (WU), whose members believed that the violent overthrow of the gov-

ernment was the only way to bring equality to repressed minorities.

The Weather Underground grew out of the anti–Vietnam War organization Students for a Democratic Society (SDS). And when the WU was formed in late 1968, it was in opposition to the war. Most members, however, expressed immediate solidarity with Black Panthers. After authorities arrested or killed dozens of Panther leaders, Weather Underground women such as Linda Evans decided to become an armed revolutionary. In 1991, Evans explained to an interviewer that she wanted to "participate in armed struggle because of the rage [she] felt after FBI/police raids on Black Panther Party

Women of the Civil Rights Movement

offices and homes ... particularly the murder of [Panther leaders] Fred Hampton and Mark Clark by Chicago police."[111]

Many Weathermen also felt that such actions by police would inevitably lead to a race war, and as Ron Jacobs writes in *The Way the Wind Blew*. "For its part, the Weathermen wanted to be on the side of the blacks. The Weathermen had given up on white people and saw the organization's role solely as one of causing chaos in support of the blacks."[112]

Although the Weather Underground was never very large—it comprised at most several thousand members nationwide—the group attracted many women. One of the founders of the organization, Bernardine Dohrn, abandoned her career as a lawyer to take up arms as a white civil rights revolutionary. Dohrn became an international symbol of revolution when her voice was heard on a May 1970 tape issued to radio stations. In the Weather Underground's "Declaration of War" against the U.S. government, Dohrn said:

Hello, I'm going to read a declaration of a state of war. ... Within the next fourteen days [the Weathermen] will attack a symbol or institution of American justice. This is the way we celebrate the example of ... all black revolutionaries who first inspired us by their fight behind enemy lines for the liberation of their people.[113]

The Weather Underground followed through with their threat. On June 9, 1970, the group set off a series of explosions in the New York City police headquarters. No one was killed, but the estimated ten to fifteen sticks of dynamite used caused the equivalent of several million dollars' worth of property damage. A communiqué issued by the group, and said to have been written by Dohrn, stated the reasons for the bombing: "The pigs in this country are our enemies. They have murdered Fred Hampton and ... are responsible for 6 black deaths in Augusta [Georgia]. ... The pigs try to look invulnerable but we keep finding their weakness."[114]

During the next five years, twenty more bombings occurred, some of them targeting high-profile targets such as the National Guard Headquarters and the United States Capitol building, both in Washington, D.C. Like other revolutionaries, Dohrn, Kathie Boudin, Naomi Jaffe, and other women of the Weather Underground were forced to assume the role of fugitives as they appeared on the FBI's "Most Wanted" lists.

Although they used violence in their attempts to change society, members of the Weather Underground took great precautions to protect human life, telephoning warnings to authorities before bombs were set to detonate. While their actions have been widely criticized,

Message to Revolutionary Women

In the August 6, 1969, issue of the *Black Panther* newspaper, Candi Robinson published a poem about revolutionary women's roles. The poem appears in the Maoist International Movement Web site's "Black Panther Newspaper Collection":

"Message to Revolutionary Women,"

Black Women, Black Women,

Hold your head up, and look ahead.

We too are needed in the revolution.

Young black women raise their fists in support of Black Power during a rally.

We too are strong. We too are a threat to the oppressive enemy. We are revolutionaries. We are the other half of our revolutionary men. We are their equal halves, may it be with gun in hand, or battling in streets to make this country a socialist lead.

Sisters, let's educate our people.

Combat . . . male chauvinism. Awaken our men to the fact that we are no more nor no less than they. We are as revolutionary as they. For too long, we have been alone. For far too long we have been women without men, for far too long we have been double oppressed, not only by the capitalist society, but also by our men. . . .

We must continue to educate our men, and bring their minds from a male chauvinistic level to a higher level.

Our men need, want and will love the beautiful children, that come from our fruitful wombs.

They need our trust and encouragement as well as we need theirs. . . .

Sisters, we are being called by life itself.

We are being called by the revolution.

We are mothers of revolutionaries, with us is the future of our people.

Dohrn, who today is a law professor at Northwestern University, defended her role in the violent organization:

I never thought violence was a good thing in a strategic sense. What happened was that I found the combination of militancy and the notion of direct action to be very compelling. . . . I thought that people who were armchair radicals . . . but weren't ready to act on their beliefs, were irrelevant and even destructive. . . . The context of the late sixties was one of tremendous official government violence, and our attempt to respond to that in an appropriate way was called by everybody "violent." . . . Ours was a very decentralized and anarchistic movement . . . the militancy remained symbolic.[115]

Symbolic or not, the activism of the late 1960s and early 1970s was unlike that of any other period in U.S. history. College students joined forces with firebrands who advocated revolution at the point of a gun. Many female revolutionaries openly advocated neutralizing police and politicians. Whether they used words, bullets, or bombs, their actions were regarded with horror and loathing by many civil rights activists who advocated peaceful change.

Many historians agree that the Weather Underground and the Black Panthers did little to improve race relations in the United States. Some even believe that their actions only frightened millions of white middle-class Americans into supporting law-and-order politicians who opposed integration, equal rights, and progressive government programs for African Americans. Whatever the case, many who survived the era continued to fight injustice where they perceived it. As Davis concludes in her autobiography: "An enormous political responsibility had been thrust upon me—I was more frightened than I had ever been in my life because I knew human lives were at stake. Our ability to keep the movement alive offered the only hope for our brothers and sisters."[116]

Chapter 7:
Creative Expressions of Protest

Songs of faith and protest have long sustained the spirits and strength of those involved in the civil rights movement. Trained to sing religious spirituals in church, women often led when voices were raised to sing protest songs such as "We Shall Overcome," "Oh, Freedom," and "We Shall Not Be Moved." These songs were sung by protesters during sit-ins, during violent confrontations with racists, while police arrested people, and in jail cells where activists were detained. They were also sung at countless funerals of women and men who were killed while fighting for equal rights.

Music played an active role in spreading the message of the civil rights movement beyond the southern battleground states. Many songs with civil rights themes such as struggle, adversity, freedom, and victory were popularized on college campuses as part of a broader folk revival, epitomized by folksingers such as Joan Baez and Odetta. These songs helped educate an entire generation of white middle-class students to the messages of hope, freedom, and triumph over adversity that made up the spiritual side of the civil rights movement. Belfrage eloquently explains the powerful role of singing at a civil rights meeting in a church in Greenwood, Mississippi:

[We] stood, everyone crossed arms, clasped hands, and sang "We Shall Overcome." . . . [We] sang out all fatigue and fear, each connected by this bond of hands to each other, communicating an infinite love and sadness. A few voices tried to harmonize, but in the end the one true tune welled up in them and overcame. It was not the song for harmony; it meant too much to change its shape for effect. All the verses were sung, and if there had been more to prolong it, it would have been prolonged, no matter how late, how tired they were. Finally the tune was hummed alone while someone spoke a prayer, and the verse struck up again, "We shall overcome," with all the voice, emo-

Civil rights activists join hands and sing in protest at the 1963 March on Washington.

tion, hope, and strength that each contained. Together [we] were an army.[117]

"They Were One"

The harmony described by Belfrage was not always in evidence in the civil rights movement. For example, there was bitter disagreement over the roles women were to play in the momentous August 1963 civil rights gathering known as the March on Washington. While planning the march, as Dorothy Height writes in *Sisters in the Struggle*, "we made it clear that we wanted to hear [a speech] from at least one woman . . . dealing with jobs and freedom. We knew, first hand, that

most of the Civil Rights Movement audiences were largely comprised of women, children, and youth."[118]

The men who ran SCLC felt that the march was about racism, not sexism, and would not allow any woman to give a speech. Women did, however, play a defining role in the entertainment that day. As an estimated 250,000 people gathered at the Washington Monument, Joan Baez started singing at 10:00 A.M., mesmerizing the crowd with "Oh, Freedom" and other civil rights songs. As David Hajdu writes in *Positively 4th Street*, Baez played the role of a major star at the march. "Ferociously earnest as well as young and unassumingly beautiful . . . [Baez] dominated the next day's [news] coverage of the entertainment program that preceded speeches by movement leaders."[119] Baez was also a star-maker, introducing the then-unknown singer/songwriter Bob Dylan to the huge crowd before performing a duet of "We Shall Overcome" with him.

Not everyone was happy to see young white singers playing such a prominent role in the march. Black activist and comedian Dick Gregory said it was fine that they supported the cause but advised them to "stand behind us—but not in front of us. . . . That would be a greater statement than arriving in their limousines and taking bows."[120] A more conciliatory opinion

Folksinger Joan Baez helped galvanize the civil rights movement through her songs of protest.

of Baez's role was offered by singer Harry Belafonte: "We were there to communicate something urgent to the power center of our culture at the time, and that power center was white. Joan . . . demonstrated with [her] participation that freedom and justice were universal concerns of import to responsible people of all colors."[121] Baez was among several women who entertained the crowd that day, singing their songs between rousing speeches by civil rights leaders. The popular African American folksinger Odetta sang the spiritual "I'm on My Way" and several other songs. Born in Birmingham, Alabama, she was the first African American woman to record black folk, work, and protest songs. In her role as interpreter of traditional music, her powerful voice and unwavering delivery ensured that she made the songs uniquely her own.

Near the end of the day, renowned gospel singer Mahalia Jackson crystallized the experience for the hundreds of thousands of marchers—and millions watching on television. Jackson performed the song "I've Been 'Buked [Rebuked] and I've Been Scorned," to the hot, tired crowd. The emotional performance prompted journalist Lerone Bennet to write:

The button-down men in front and the old women in back came to their feet screaming and shouting. They had not known that this [emotion] was in them, and that they wanted it touched. From different places and different ways, with different dreams they had come, and now, hearing this sung, they were one.[122]

After this defining moment, Jackson requested that the crowd sing with her the spiritual "How I Got Over." As the song ended and the last voices died down, Martin Luther King Jr. took the podium and delivered his transcendent "I Have a Dream" speech.

"I Had Gotten the Spirit"

The women who sang at the March on Washington played many roles in the civil rights movement before and after that day. Baez, for example, was already a celebrated singer in 1961, and she was barely aware of the movement the first time she toured the South. She noticed, however, that there were no African Americans at any of her concerts. When she discovered that segregation laws kept them from the concert hall, Baez used her celebrity to insist in her contracts that her concerts be integrated. By this time she was singing civil rights protest songs, and she decided to break racial boundaries, holding concerts at four black colleges in the Deep South. But the tour was to be more than a musical experience. Baez wanted to learn as much as possible about the civil rights movement as well as participate in it.

In 1963, before her scheduled concert in Birmingham, Baez arrived several days early to tour the troubled city with King and other activists. She attended a sermon, called "Singing at Midnight," in which music played an important role. People stood up, one by one, and talked about going to jail for protesting. In this emotional setting, Baez was weeping when the preacher asked her to sing for the crowd. In her memoir, *And a Voice to Sing With*, Baez describes her transformation from folksinger to her new role as soul singer:

Folks mumbled and shifted around ... [as I] went up to the pulpit. I started in singing "Let Us Break Bread Together on Our Knees," and folks joined in. I sang in a voice very different from the pure white one which is on all my records. I sang with the soul I was adopting right there in that room, and heads began to nod in approval, and wrinkled old faces smiled in confusion and pleasure. Then I sang "Swing Low," and folks started to get happy. Handkerchiefs came out and fans doubled their speed. A couple of folks yelled out "UHHUH, LAWD!" and then one old lady in a magenta hat went [fainted from the emotion] and had to be carried out, and I was scared but I kept on singing, because, I suppose you might say, I had gotten the spirit.[123]

The next day, as hundreds of Birmingham civil rights activists were being clubbed, teargassed, and arrested by police, Baez was scheduled to play at Miles College. As the auditorium on the all-black campus filled, the ability of Baez's music to cross racial barriers was evident. As one observer stated as he saw black and white sitting side by side: "This is the first time whites have ever stepped foot onta this campus."[124] Baez did her show and finished with "We Shall Overcome." She describes the scene: "[The] audience rose and held hands, swaying back and forth while they sang. The singing was soft and tentative and many people were crying. . . . [A journalist who was there] said that the concert had an overwhelming impact on her life. And so it did on mine."[125]

The Free Southern Theater

While protests were carried out to the sounds of music, women of the civil rights movement utilized other methods of creative expression to educate the public and voice their opposition to racism and segregation. During the 1960s, a growing base of actors, writers, and directors were inspired to incorporate pressing social issues such as civil rights and racism into their work. They formed their own theatrical companies, broadly known as alternative theater, set in storefronts, garages, warehouses, or even parking lots and street corners.

One such venue, the Free Southern Theater, was formed in Mississippi in late 1963 by Doris Derby, Denise Nicholas, and playwrights Gilbert Moses and John O'Neal. Derby was a founding member of the New York chapter of SNCC, a major civil rights fund-raiser who utilized art and artists to attract donors, and an educator who taught adults to read. In *Women in the Civil Rights Movement*, Clarissa Myrick-Harris explains that Derby went beyond the traditional roles expected from women at that time:

[When Derby moved South] to help develop an experimental adult literacy program at Tougaloo College in Mississippi, she continued her flexible activism, transcending the roles that black males thought should determine the tenor and tone of her contributions. On the one hand, Derby's decision to help set up this program can be viewed as an understandable decision made by an educator. Such a role seems consistent with the traditional role of schoolteacher that many would associate with black women. On the other hand, the decision to practice her profession in an environment where the worth and humanity of her pupils—African-American—were not acknowledged and where the penalties for being an educated African-American ranged from ostracism to murder meant that Derby was moving beyond the traditional role of educator to that of liberator.[126]

Derby combined her skills as an edu-cator and organizer with her creativity and talent when she cofounded the Free Southern Theater. The goal of the theater was not only to entertain but also to educate its black southern audience about

"Keep Your Eyes on the Prize"

During Freedom Summer in 1964, most white middle-class civil rights volunteers heard African American songs of protest for the first time. In *Freedom Summer*, Sally Belfrage describes the first musical encounter between civil rights activist Fannie Lou Hamer and a group of white college students headed into a summer of danger in the South where they would try to register black voters:

Mrs. Fannie Lou Hamer was suddenly leading [the chorus]. . . .

If you miss me from the back of the bus,
You can't find me nowhere,
Come on up to the front of the bus,
I'll be ridin' up there. . . .

Her voice gave everything she had, and her circle soon incorporated . . . others, expanding first in size and in volume and then something else—it gained passion. Few of them knew who she was, and in her plump, perspiring face many could probably see something of the woman who cleaned their mothers' floors at home. But here was clearly someone with force enough for all of them, who knew the meaning of "Oh Freedom" and "We Shall Not Be Moved" in her flesh and spirit as they never would. They lost their shyness and began to sing the choruses with abandon, though their voices all together dimmed beside hers.

Paul and Silas, bound in jail,
Had no money for to go their bail,
Keep your eyes on the prize,
Hold on, hold on.

"Hold on," they bellowed back, "Hold o-o-on. Keep your eyes on the prize, hold on." The music had begun—the music that would have to take the place for them, all summer, of swimming, solitude, sex, movies, walking, drinking, driving, or any of the releases they had ever grown to need; and would somehow have to come to mean enough to drive off fear.

Women's Role in "We Shall Overcome"

❧

"We Shall Overcome" was the anthem of the civil rights movement in the early 1960s. Although the song was based on an old spiritual, women played important roles in transforming it into a song of protest, strength, and victory. Folksinger Pete Seeger explains on the "We Shall Overcome" Web site by Henry Kochlin:

In 1946 several hundred employees of the American Tobacco Company in Charleston, S.C., were on strike. Most were women, most African-Americans. To keep their spirits up, they often sang hymns on the picket line. Lucille Simmons especially liked to sing [Charles Tindley's 1900 gospel song "I'll Overcome Some Day"] but she sang it very, very slowly. . . . And Lucille changed one important word, from "I" to "we."

Zilphia Horton, a white woman, learned it when a group of strikers visited the Highlander Folk School, the labor education center in Tennessee. Zilphia also had a beautiful alto voice, and she also sang it very slowly. It became her favorite song. She taught it to me. So we published

it as "We Will Overcome" in our little song newsletter, 'People's Song.' . . .

No one is sure who changed "will" to "shall." . . . But Septima Clark, a Charleston schoolteacher (who was director of education at Highlander) . . . always preferred "shall." It sings better.

A civil rights activist at the 1963 March on Washington sings the movement's anthem with feeling.

Women of the Civil Rights Movement

African American history and the civil rights movement.

Although the Free Southern Theater had noble goals, Derby clashed with the male leadership. While she used her artistic talent to design sets and paint theatrical backdrops, the men expected her to type, file, and take care of the theater's bookkeeping. Derby ignored these traditional roles, however, stating: "I was going to do what I wanted to do no matter what they thought."[127] When Moses and O'Neal decided to move the Free Southern Theater to New Orleans in 1965, Derby chose to stay in the heart of the civil rights movement in Mississippi. She continued her work as educator and artist, however, teaching adult literacy and using her camera to photograph the lives of black people in rural southern counties.

Strong Foundations

When the Free Southern Theater left Mississippi, Denise Nicholas moved, too. Nicholas did not have a strong background in the civil rights movement. And she initially came to the theater by working as an actress, script reader, and office worker, and as the wife of Gilbert Moses. Although she was one of the founding members of the theater, Nicholas was willing to take on the roles assigned to her because, as she later recalled: "I was not as strong as I am now. . . . Then I was able to be led because I was so young and ignorant about so many things."[128]

While that may have been the case, Nicholas risked her life as an actress with the Free Southern Theater. One play she was in, Martin Duberman's *In White America*, had great educational value as a work about different aspects of African American history. Featuring an integrated cast, it angered white supremacists who bombed the theater during a performance in McComb, Mississippi. While frightened, Nicholas continued with the presentation, later recalling: "You just keep going. . . . It's like being in the trenches and testing yourself. In a way you are in the process of developing and growing into what you want to be as a human being and those kinds of situations of danger help you find yourself."[129]

Nicholas continued to define herself by learning about black nationalism and Black Power. When the theater moved to New Orleans, Nicholas became a community educator, setting up a library, the Afro-American/African Information Center, inside the Free Southern Theater. The materials within the library were meant to educate young men and women about black history and politics. As Nicholas stated: "I wanted to see little children walk with their heads up high, reading Negro history, understanding fully this bind Whitey put us in."[130]

By 1967, Nicholas was eager to get back to her first love, theater. She moved to New York and continued with her dual roles of performer and educator, taking acting roles that she felt shone a positive light on the African American experience. In later years she became a national star, acting in dozens of movies and television shows. Nicholas was also a scriptwriter, writing for several hit TV shows.

Nicholas and Derby took on different jobs in the Free Southern Theater, but, as Myrick-Harris writes, the women achieved similar goals in the end:

> The roles each woman played behind the scenes and on the frontlines of the movement while involved with the [Free Southern Theater] validate the idea that African-American women contribute most to their own development and the development of African America when they step out of roles defined for them by black men and step into roles informed by both their personal experiences and an appreciation of their racial heritage. For Derby her experience in the Free Southern Theater affirmed her decisions to contribute to the movement by creating and implementing educational and community programs in Mississippi. Her decade of work in Mississippi, in turn, provided a strong foundation for her

current work as a director of the Minority Information Center for the University of Wisconsin system. For Nicholas the Theater provided an intense training ground that has enriched her life and informed her career in theater, television, and film.[131]

A Raisin in the Sun

The audience for the Free Southern Theater was largely African American, and during the 1960s few black women had the opportunity to educate white America about civil rights. Lorraine Hansberry, however, was able to use her talents as

Playwright Lorraine Hansberry's A Raisin in the Sun *was the first play by an African American woman to be produced on Broadway.*

a playwright to show white audiences the reality of life for poverty-stricken African Americans.

Hansberry drew on personal experience in her writing. She was born in Chicago in 1930 and grew up in a relatively prosperous black family. Hansberry's father made his money as a real estate broker in segregated Chicago where black tenants or home owners were barred from white areas. When Hansberry was eight, in order to challenge these restrictions, her father bought a house in a segregated white neighborhood and moved in with his family. A mob attacked the house and threw a brick through one of the windows. The horrors Hansberry encountered in the weeks that followed are detailed in her autobiography, *To Be Young, Gifted, and Black*: "My memories . . . include being spat at, cursed, and pummeled in my daily trek to and from school."[132]

While Hansberry was terrorized by these incidents, in later years she was able to interpret these events in a creative way. Her most famous play, *A Raisin in the Sun*, is about a black family who gets a large sum of money from an insurance settlement and moves to a white neighborhood.

In her role as playwright, Hansberry wrote about the African American experience in an artistic way. Rather than preach a specific message or portray black characters in stereotypical roles, she created situations that were painful in their realism. In *A Raisin in the Sun*, characters argued, mumbled, and displayed human frailties that were unusual in the largely optimistic plays written in the mid-1950s. As Hansberry wrote to her mother: "Mama, it is a play that tells the truth about people, Negroes and life and I think it will help a lot of people to understand how we are just as complicated as they are . . . people who are the very essence of human dignity."[133]

When *A Raisin in the Sun* was completed in 1958, Hansberry had to become a saleswoman and fund-raiser in her attempts to get the play produced. No one, it seemed, wanted to risk money on a play with an all-black cast that dealt with controversial, racially sensitive concepts. However, when the play finally made it to New York City's Broadway— the theater capital of the United States— it was greeted with great enthusiasm by audiences and critics alike.

With this achievement, at the age of twenty-nine, Hansberry entered the record books. She was the first black woman to have a play produced on Broadway. When *Raisin* won the prestigious New York Drama Critics' Circle Award for best play of the year, she was the first woman and the first African American recipient. She was also the youngest recipient of the award, a title she still holds. Hansberry's groundbreaking achievement is summed up by critic David Littlejohn: "It would

To Kill a Mockingbird

❦

With a few exceptions, the painful stories about the racism and poverty faced by African Americans were rarely mentioned in the pages of popular books. One exception, however, was *To Kill a Mockingbird*, a fictional story based on the reality of life in a small town in Alabama. Published in 1960 by white southern author Harper Lee, the novel is told from the viewpoint of a young girl nicknamed Scout who, wise beyond her years, describes the racism and prejudice around her.

Although Lee never wrote another novel, *To Kill a Mockingbird* broke dozens of records. It was chosen by three American book clubs, sold more than 2.5 million copies the first year, and went through fourteen printings. On the second anniversary of its publication, *Mockingbird* had been on the best-seller lists for one hundred weeks and had sold more than 5 million copies in thirteen countries. Lee was awarded the Pulitzer Prize in Letters on May 1, 1961. The book was made into a film in 1962 and won three Oscars. In her role as best-selling author, Lee shunned publicity, however. She let the work speak for itself and rarely gave interviews. *To Kill a Mockingbird* remains a classic that is studied in classrooms throughout the world.

not be unfair in dating the emergence of a serious and mature Negro theater in America from 1959, the date of Lorraine Hansberry's *A Raisin in the Sun*."[134]

Hansberry was also a prolific writer of essays, film scripts, and a novel based roughly on her life. When she was diagnosed with cancer in 1963, Hansberry battled on, writing through chemotherapy treatment. Even after she became ill, she played an important role in the civil rights movement, working as a fund-raiser for SNCC and meeting with Attorney General Robert Kennedy to discuss integration and racism.

When Hansberry died at the age of thirty-four in early January 1965, she left several plays unfinished. Her influence continued after her death, however. The play that changed American theater forever ran for nearly two years on Broadway and has been produced innumerable times since its premiere. *A Raisin in the Sun* was made into a film in 1961, adapted into a Tony Award–winning musical in 1973, and produced for television in 1989.

Hansberry took on many roles in her journey as an artist. Like Baez, Derby, Nicholas, and other creative women, her art and her emotional strength spread the ideals of the civil rights movement to millions of people throughout the United States—and the world.

Notes

Introduction:
Fighting for Racial Equality

1. Quoted in I.F. Stone, *The Haunted Fifties*. New York: Random House, 1969, p. 61.
2. Quoted in Bettye Collier-Thomas and V.P. Franklin, eds., *Sisters in the Struggle*. New York: New York University Press, 2001, p. 90.
3. Malcolm X and Alex Haley, *The Autobiography of Malcolm X*. New York: Ballantine, 1990, p. 226.
4. Quoted in Collier-Thomas and Franklin, *Sisters in the Struggle*, p. 91.

Chapter 1: Women in Civil Rights Organizations

5. Steven F. Lawson, *Civil Rights Crossroads*. Lexington: University of Kentucky Press, 2003, pp. 265–66.
6. Quoted in Lynne Olson, *Freedom's Daughters*. New York: Scribner, 2001, p. 141.
7. Lawson, *Civil Rights Crossroads*, p. 267.
8. Jo Ann Gibson Robinson, *The Montgomery Bus Boycott and the Women Who Started It*. Knoxville: University of Tennessee Press, 1987, p. 23.
9. Quoted in Belinda Robnett, *How Long? How Long?* New York: Oxford University Press, 1997, p. 56.
10. Quoted in Vicki L. Crawford, Jacqueline Anne Rouse, and Barbara Woods, eds., *Women in the Civil Rights Movement*. Brooklyn: Carlson, 1990, p. 57.
11. Quoted in Barbara Ransby, *Ella Baker and the Black Freedom Movement*. Chapel Hill: University of North Carolina Press, 2003, p. 114.
12. Quoted in Ransby, *Ella Baker and the Black Freedom Movement*, p. 116.
13. Ransby, *Ella Baker and the Black Freedom Movement*, p. 105.
14. Quoted in Steve Levin, "Daisy Lampkin Was a Dynamo for Change," *Pittsburgh Post-Gazette*, February 2, 1998. www.post-gazette.com/blackhistory month/19980202lampkin.asp.
15. J. Douglas Allen-Taylor, "Septima Clark: Teacher to a Movement," Safero (no date). www.safero.org/articles/septima.html.
16. Quoted in Robnett, *How Long? How Long?* p. 94.
17. Quoted in Robnett, *How Long? How Long?* p. 94.
18. Septima Clark, "Transcript #17, Oral History Project," Atlanta: Martin Luther King Center, p. 39.
19. Quoted in Robnett, *How Long? How Long?* p. 95.
20. Quoted in Zita Allen, *Black Women Leaders of the Civil Rights*

Movement. New York: Franklin Watts, 1996, p. 69.

21. Quoted in Crawford, Rouse, and Woods, *Women in the Civil Rights Movement,* pp. 2–3.

22. "Student Nonviolent Coordinating Committee," Martin Luther King Papers Project, 2002. www.stanford.edu/group/King/about_king/encyclopedia/enc_SNCC.htm.

23. Debra L. Schultz, *Going South: Jewish Women in the Civil Rights Movement.* New York: New York University Press, 2001, p. 13.

24. Schultz, *Going South: Jewish Women in the Civil Rights Movement,* p. 35.

25. Schultz, *Going South: Jewish Women in the Civil Rights Movement,* p. 35.

26. Quoted in Olson, *Freedom's Daughters,* p. 170.

27. Quoted in Shirley Abbott, *Womenfolks: Growing Up Down South.* New York: Ticknor and Fields, 1983, p. 201.

28. Quoted in Olson, *Freedom's Daughters,* p. 170.

29. Quoted in Olson, *Freedom's Daughters,* p. 171.

Chapter 2:
Protesting Segregation

30. Quoted in Collier-Thomas and Franklin, *Sisters in the Struggle,* p. 19.

31. Rosa Parks, *Rosa Parks: My Story.* New York: Dial, 1992, p. 116.

32. Robinson, *The Montgomery Bus Boycott and the Women Who Started It,* pp. 45–46.

33. Robinson, *The Montgomery Bus Boycott and the Women Who Started It,* p. 47.

34. Quoted in Robinson, *The Montgomery Bus Boycott and the Women Who Started It,* p. 60.

35. Quoted in Robinson, *The Montgomery Bus Boycott and the Women Who Started It,* p. 164.

36. Deborah Gray White, *Too Heavy a Load.* New York: W.W. Norton, 1999, pp. 179–80.

37. Allen, *Black Women Leaders of the Civil Rights Movement,* p. 72.

38. Olson, *Freedom's Daughters,* p. 157.

39. Quoted in Olson, *Freedom's Daughters,* p. 158.

40. Quoted in Olson, *Freedom's Daughters,* p. 156.

41. Quoted in Robnett, *How Long? How Long?* p. 104.

42. Quoted in Robnett, *How Long? How Long?* p. 104.

43. Olson, *Freedom's Daughters,* p. 186.

44. Schultz, *Going South: Jewish Women in the Civil Rights Movement,* p. 39.

45. Quoted in Schultz, *Going South: Jewish Women in the Civil Rights Movement,* p. 42.

46. Quoted in Schultz, *Going South: Jewish Women in the Civil Rights Movement,* p. 42.

Chapter 3:
Fighting for an Education

47. Quoted in Collier-Thomas and

Franklin, *Sisters in the Struggle*, pp. 108–109.

48. Septima Clark, *Ready from Within*. Navarro, CA: Wild Trees, 1986, p. 64.
49. Clark, *Ready from Within*, p. 50.
50. Quoted in Olson, *Freedom's Daughters*, p. 214.
51. Quoted in Collier-Thomas and Franklin, *Sisters in the Struggle*, p. 114.
52. Quoted in Collier-Thomas and Franklin, *Sisters in the Struggle*, p. 114.
53. Quoted in Olson, *Freedom's Daughters*, p. 137.
54. Quoted in Olson, *Freedom's Daughters*, p. 135.
55. "Melba Pattillo Beals 1998 Interview," Scholastic, 1998. http://teacher.scholastic.com/barrier/hwyf/mpbstory/melchat.htm.
56. Lawson, *Civil Rights Crossroads*, p. 272.
57. Carolyn Calloway-Thomas and Thurmon Garner, "Daisy Bates and the Little Rock Crisis: Forging the Way," *Journal of Black Studies*, 1996, pp. 623–24.
58. Charlayne Hunter-Gault and Mary Marshall Clark, "Interview," Washington Press Club Foundation, June 15, 1993. http://womenshistory.about.com/gi/dynamic/offsite.htm?site=http%3A%2F%2Fnpc.press.org%2Fwpforal%2 Fhunt1.htm.
59. Quoted in Charlayne Hunter-Gault, *In My Place*. New York: Vintage, 1992, p. 129.
60. Quoted in Hunter-Gault, *In My Place*, p. 171.
61. Hunter-Gault, *In My Place*, p. 172.
62. Hunter-Gault, *In My Place*, p. 182.
63. Hunter-Gault, *In My Place*, p. 183.
64. "Melba Pattillo Beals 1998 Interview."

Chapter 4:
Expanding Voting Rights

65. Quoted in Crawford, Rouse, and Woods, *Women in the Civil Rights Movement*, p. 17.
66. Quoted in Sally Belfrage, *Freedom Summer*. New York: Viking, 1965, p. 21.
67. Quoted in Chana Kai Lee, *For Freedom's Sake: The Life of Fannie Lou Hamer*. Chicago: University of Illinois Press, 1999, p. 39.
68. Quoted in "Fannie Lou Hamer 1917–1977," Minerva Computer Services, 1997. www.beejae.com/hamer.htm.
69. Crawford, Rouse, and Woods, *Women in the Civil Rights Movement*, p. 19.
70. Quoted in Crawford, Rouse, and Woods, *Women in the Civil Rights Movement*, p. 20.
71. Doug McAdam, *Freedom Summer*. New York: Oxford University Press, 1988, p. 39.
72. Quoted in McAdam, *Freedom Summer*, p. 59.
73. Quoted in McAdam, *Freedom Summer*, p. 68.
74. Quoted in Juan Williams, *Eyes on the Prize: America's Civil Rights Years, 1954–1965*. New York: Viking Penguin, 1987, p. 230.

75. Belfrage, *Freedom Summer*, p. 17.
76. Belfrage, *Freedom Summer*, p. 23.
77. Quoted in Olson, *Freedom's Daughters*, p. 297.
78. Belfrage, *Freedom Summer*, pp. 195–96.
79. Quoted in Sara Evans, *Personal Politics*. New York: Vintage, 1980, p. 71.
80. Quoted in Evans, *Personal Politics*, p. 75.
81. Belfrage, *Freedom Summer*, p. 103.

Chapter 5:
Women in Political Office

82. Quoted in Collier-Thomas and Franklin, *Sisters in the Struggle*, p. 306.
83. Quoted in Joanne Grant, "Way of Life in Mississippi," *National Guardian*, February 13, 1964, p. 12.
84. Quoted in Kay Mills, *This Little Light of Mine: The Life of Fannie Lou Hamer*. New York: Dutton, 1993, p. 121.
85. Quoted in Lee, *For Freedom's Sake: The Life of Fannie Lou Hamer*, p. 109.
86. Lee, *For Freedom's Sake: The Life of Fannie Lou Hamer*, p. 108.
87. Quoted in Lee, *For Freedom's Sake: The Life of Fannie Lou Hamer*, p. 114.
88. Quoted in Collier-Thomas and Franklin, *Sisters in the Struggle*, p. 134.
89. Quoted in Lawson, *Civil Rights Crossroads*, p. 110.
90. Shirley Chisholm, *Unbought and Unbossed*. Boston: Houghton Mifflin, 1970, p. 48.
91. Chisholm, *Unbought and Unbossed*, p. 71.
92. Chisholm, *Unbought and Unbossed*, p. 69.
93. Chisholm, *Unbought and Unbossed*, p. 104.
94. Quoted in Mary Beth Rogers, *Barbara Jordan American Hero*. New York: Bantam, 2000, p. 111.
95. Quoted in Rogers, *Barbara Jordan American Hero*, p. 111.
96. Quoted in Rogers, *Barbara Jordan American Hero*, p. 115.
97. Quoted in Rogers, *Barbara Jordan American Hero*, p. 214.
98. Quoted in Rogers, *Barbara Jordan American Hero*, p. 265.

Chapter 6:
Radicals and Militants

99. Quoted in Collier-Thomas and Franklin, *Sisters in the Struggle*, p. 198.
100. Quoted in Collier-Thomas and Franklin, *Sisters in the Struggle*, p. 198.
101. Quoted in Cynthia Griggs Fleming, *Soon We Will Not Cry*. New York: Rowman & Littlefield, 1998, pp. 135–36.
102. Evans, *Personal Politics*, pp. 88–89.
103. Fleming, *Soon We Will Not Cry*, p. 167.
104. Quoted in Collier-Thomas and Franklin, *Sisters in the Struggle*, p. 204.
105. Quoted in Collier-Thomas and Franklin, *Sisters in the Struggle*, p. 208.
106. Quoted in J.A. Parker, *Angela Davis: The Making of a Revolutionary*. New

Rochelle, NY: Arlington House, 1973, p. 93.

107. Elaine Brown, *A Taste of Power*. New York: Pantheon, 1992, pp. 136–37.

108. Quoted in Brown, *A Taste of Power*, p. 140.

109. Brown, *A Taste of Power*, p. 275.

110. Brown, *A Taste of Power*, p. 357.

111. Quoted in Ron Jacobs, *The Way the Wind Blew*. New York: Verso, 1997, p. 86.

112. Jacobs, *The Way the Wind Blew*, pp. 86–87.

113. Quoted in Thomas P. Raynor, *Terrorism: Past, Present, Future*. New York: Franklin Watts, 1982, p. 71.

114. Quoted in Jacobs, *The Way the Wind Blew*, pp. 110–11.

115. Quoted in Ron Chepesiuk, *Sixties Radicals, Then and Now*. Jefferson, NC: McFarland, 1995, p. 235.

116. Angela Davis, *Angela Davis: An Autobiography*. New York: Random House, 1974, p. 398.

Chapter 7:
Creative Expressions of Protest

117. Belfrage, *Freedom Summer*, p. 55.

118. Quoted in Collier-Thomas and Franklin, *Sisters in the Struggle*, p. 86.

119. David Hajdu, *Positively 4th Street*. New York: North Point, 2001, p. 182.

120. Quoted in Hajdu, *Positively 4th Street*, p. 183.

121. Quoted in Hajdu, *Positively 4th Street*, p. 183.

122. Quoted in Doris E. Saunders, ed., *The Day They Marched*. Chicago:

Johnson, 1963, p. 12.

123. Joan Baez, *And a Voice to Sing With*. New York: New American Library, 1987, p. 104.

124. Quoted in Baez, *And a Voice to Sing With*, p. 106.

125. Baez, *And a Voice to Sing With*, p. 106.

126. Quoted in Crawford, Rouse, and Woods, *Women in the Civil Rights Movement*, pp. 220–21.

127. Quoted in Crawford, Rouse, and Woods, *Women in the Civil Rights Movement*, p. 224.

128. Quoted in Crawford, Rouse, and Woods, *Women in the Civil Rights Movement*, p. 226.

129. Quoted in Crawford, Rouse, and Woods, *Women in the Civil Rights Movement*, p. 226.

130. Quoted in Thomas C. Dent, Richard Schechner, and Gilbert Moses, *The Free Southern Theater by the Free Southern Theater*. New York: Bobbs-Merrill, 1967, pp. 184–85.

131. Quoted in Crawford, Rouse, and Woods, *Women in the Civil Rights Movement,* p. 231.

132. Lorraine Hansberry, *To Be Young, Gifted, and Black*. New York: Vintage, 1995, p. 21.

133. Quoted in Walter French, ed., *Lorraine Hansberry*. Boston: Twayne, 1984, p. 55.

134. Quoted in French, *Lorraine Hansberry*, p. 55.

For Further Reading

Books

Maria Fleming, ed., *A Place at the Table: Struggles for Equality in America*. New York: Oxford University Press, 2001. Examines the efforts of many different people in American history to secure equal treatment in such areas as religion, voting rights, education, housing, and employment.

James Haskins, *Power to the People: The Rise and Fall of the Black Panther Party*. New York: Simon & Schuster, 1997. Chronicles the history of the Black Panther Party, the radical political organization founded in 1966 by Huey Newton and Bobby Seale, which promoted armed revolution against racist law enforcement authorities.

Charlayne Hunter-Gault, *In My Place*. New York: Vintage, 1992. The autobiography of the woman who desegregated the University of Georgia and went on to become a national correspondent for the MacNeil News Hour on PBS.

Laura Baskes Litwin, *Fannie Lou Hamer: Fighting for the Right to Vote*. Berkeley Heights, NJ: Enslow, 2002. A biography of the civil rights activist who devoted her life to helping blacks register to vote.

Cookie Lommel, *Mary Church Terrell*. Berkeley Heights, NJ: Enslow, 2003. A biography of the activist who was the first black woman to earn a college degree, who was the first president of the National Association of Colored Women, and who organized sit-ins at lunch counters at the age of eighty-six.

Web Sites

"Black Panther Newspaper Collection," MIM, 2004. www.etext.org/Politics/MIM/bpp/. A Web site that links some of the original writings of the Black Panther Party from its first three years of existence when it grew to be an explosive power in America.

"The Civil Rights Era," African American Odyssey, March 15, 2002. http://lcweb2.loc.gov/ammem/aao html/exhibit/aopart9.html. A site maintained by the Library of Congress with various source photos, letters, newspaper clippings, documents, and other media concerning the civil rights movement. Includes photos of the Little Rock Nine, letters from Daisy Bates to the NAACP, and headlines from the Montgomery bus boycott.

"Culture and Change: Black History in America," Scholastic, 2004. http://teacher.scholastic.com/activities/bhistory/index.htm. A site with links to biographies of famous African American civil rights activists including Rosa Parks, Melba Pattillo, and others.

Dorothy Height, "Open Wide the Freedom Gates," Online NewsHour. http://spod.cx/s?747. The legend of the civil rights movement and former head of the National Council of Negro Women talks about her life on a Web site that provides links to written, audio, and visual stories concerning women and civil rights.

"On the Front Lines with the Little Rock 9," PBS Kids, 2004. http://pbskids.org/wayback/civilrights/features_school.html. A site with details of the Little Rock Nine desegregation case at Central High with links to photos and an interview with Melba Beals.

Works Consulted

Books

Shirley Abbott, *Womenfolks: Growing Up Down South.* New York: Ticknor and Fields, 1983. A blend of history, memoir, and political essay taken from diaries and journals of early southern immigrants and visitors, family stories, academic histories of the South, and southern historical fiction.

Zita Allen, *Black Women Leaders of the Civil Rights Movement.* New York: Franklin Watts, 1996. Biographies of women who led the fight for black rights throughout the twentieth century.

Joan Baez, *And a Voice to Sing With.* New York: New American Library, 1987. The memoir of a singer known as the Queen of Folk whose passion for equal rights and nonviolence placed her at the center of dozens of civil rights marches and antiwar rallies.

Sally Belfrage, *Freedom Summer.* New York: Viking, 1965. An eyewitness account from a white middle-class college student who volunteered to brave intimidation and violence in order to promote black voter registration in Mississippi in 1964.

Elaine Brown, *A Taste of Power.* New York: Pantheon, 1992. The autobiography of a Black Panther leader who confronted racism, sexism, and radical politics during the late civil rights era.

Ellen Cantarow, *Moving the Mountain.* Old Westbury, NY: Feminist Press, 1980. An oral history of three women activists, Florence Luscomb who campaigned for women's suffrage, Ella Baker who led civil rights organizations, and Jessie Lopen De La Cruz who organized farmworkers.

Clayborne Carson, *In Struggle.* Cambridge: Harvard University Press, 1981. The history and ideology of the Student Nonviolent Coordinating Committee, an organization founded by black college students and guided by Ella Baker.

Ron Chepesiuk, *Sixties Radicals, Then and Now.* Jefferson, NC: McFarland, 1995. Interviews with sixties activists who helped shape the antiwar and civil rights debate; provides an interesting perspective of radicals looking back from the 1990s.

Shirley Chisholm, *Unbought and Unbossed.* Boston: Houghton Mifflin, 1970. The autobiography of the first black woman to serve in the United States Congress, written only two years after she was elected.

Septima Clark, *Ready from Within*. Navarro, CA: Wild Trees, 1986. An autobiographical narrative from the woman who set up Citizenship Schools throughout the South so black people could learn to read.

Bettye Collier-Thomas and V.P. Franklin, eds., *Sisters in the Struggle*. New York: New York University Press, 2001. A collection of sixteen essays by African American women who actively participated in the civil rights and Black Power movements.

Vicki L. Crawford, Jacqueline Anne Rouse, and Barbara Woods, eds., *Women in the Civil Rights Movement*. Brooklyn: Carlson, 1990. A title in a sixteen-volume series, Black Women in United States History, this book contains detailed biographies of many renowned black women who participated in the civil rights movement between 1945 and 1965.

Angela Davis, *Angela Davis: An Autobiography*. New York: Random House, 1974. The life story of a woman who was a Black Panther, a Communist, a fugitive, and a college professor.

Thomas C. Dent, Richard Schechner, and Gilbert Moses, *The Free Southern Theater by the Free Southern Theater*. New York: Bobbs-Merrill, 1967. A history of the theater that produced plays focusing on black history and black empowerment by those who worked with the theater.

Sara Evans, *Personal Politics*. New York: Vintage, 1980. A study of the sexism rampant in the civil rights and New Left movements and how this mistreatment of women led to the women's liberation movement of the late 1960s.

Bryna J. Fireside, *Is There a Woman in the House . . . or Senate?* Morton Grove, IL: Albert Whitman, 1994. Biographies of ten women who served in Congress, including Shirley Chisholm, Barbara Jordan, and other African American women.

Cynthia Griggs Fleming, *Soon We Will Not Cry*. New York: Rowman & Littlefield, 1998. A biography of civil rights activist and SNCC leader Ruby Doris Smith Robinson.

Walter French, ed., *Lorraine Hansberry*. Boston: Twayne, 1984. A comprehensive exploration of the life and works of the famous black playwright whose powerful works educated white audiences to the realities of African American life.

David Hajdu, *Positively 4th Street*. New York: North Point, 2001. The lives and times of four seminal figures in the American folk music scene, covering the experiences of Joan Baez,

Bob Dylan, Mimi Baez Fariña, and Richard Fariña up to 1965.

Lorraine Hansberry, *To Be Young, Gifted, and Black*. New York: Vintage, 1995. Hansberry's life from a childhood in Chicago to the world's most celebrated black playwright, taken from letters, interviews, and autobiographical writings after the author's death.

Ron Jacobs, *The Way the Wind Blew*. New York: Verso, 1997. A concise history of the Weather Underground, a group that protested the Vietnam War and racism by planting bombs in banks, military installations, and even the United States Capitol.

Barbara Jordan and Shelby Hearon, *Barbara Jordan: A Self-Portrait*. Garden City, NY: Doubleday, 1979. The autobiography of the first black woman elected to the Texas senate in the twentieth century who went on to become the first African American woman from the South to be elected to Congress.

Steven F. Lawson, *Civil Rights Crossroads*. Lexington: University of Kentucky Press, 2003. A compilation of articles written by the author over a twenty-five-year time span that chronicle the struggles for voting rights and other issues central to the civil rights movement.

Chana Kai Lee, *For Freedom's Sake: The Life of Fannie Lou Hamer*. Chicago: University of Illinois Press, 1999. The life and times of one of the most revered civil rights activists of the 1960s.

Malcolm X and Alex Haley, *The Autobiography of Malcolm X*. New York: Ballantine, 1990. The life story of one of the most famous and charismatic leaders of the Black Power revolution.

Doug McAdam, *Freedom Summer*. New York: Oxford University Press, 1988. The story of over one thousand black and white college students who risked arrests, beatings, and death to register black voters in the South in the summer of 1964.

Kay Mills, *This Little Light of Mine: The Life of Fannie Lou Hamer*. New York: Dutton, 1993. A biography of the women who challenged Mississippi racism, registered to vote against the odds, ran for Congress, and founded a political party.

Lynne Olson, *Freedom's Daughters*. New York: Scribner, 2001. Historical and biographical information about women who fought for civil rights between 1830 and 1970.

J.A. Parker, *Angela Davis: The Making of a Revolutionary*. New Rochelle, NY: Arlington House, 1973. A biography of the sixties revolutionary with an emphasis on the life experiences that drove her to political activism.

Rosa Parks, *Rosa Parks: My Story*. New York: Dial, 1992. The autobiography of the woman who started the Montgomery bus boycott when she refused to give up her bus seat to a white man.

Barbara Ransby, *Ella Baker and the Black Freedom Movement*. Chapel Hill: University of North Carolina Press, 2003. A biography of one of the most important civil rights leaders of the twentieth century whose work spanned over fifty years.

Thomas P. Raynor, *Terrorism: Past, Present, Future*. New York: Franklin Watts, 1982. Discusses various forms of terrorism including the execution of Marie Antoinette in the French Revolution in the late eighteenth century, the violent acts of sixties revolutionaries, and problems of terrorism in the early 1980s.

Jo Ann Gibson Robinson, *The Montgomery Bus Boycott and the Women Who Started It*. Knoxville: University of Tennessee Press, 1987. Women were the prime movers behind the historic boycott that marked the beginning of the end of segregation in the South. The author was one of the prime organizers behind the scenes.

Belinda Robnett, *How Long? How Long?* New York: Oxford University Press, 1997. A scholarly look at black women's roles in the grassroots leadership of the civil rights movement.

Mary Beth Rogers, *Barbara Jordan American Hero*. New York: Bantam, 2000. A biography of the Texas senator and congresswoman who broke racial barriers in order to further the cause of civil rights in the United States.

Doris E. Saunders, ed., *The Day They Marched*. Chicago: Johnson, 1963. Account of the civil rights march of August 28, 1963, in Washington, D.C., including statements of President Kennedy, Martin Luther King, and many others who were there.

Debra L. Schultz, *Going South: Jewish Women in the Civil Rights Movement*. New York: New York University Press, 2001. An oral history of more than a dozen women who left their comfortable middle-class homes, their college classes, and their promising careers to risk their lives in the fight for racial equality.

Susan Stern, *With the Weathermen*. Garden City, NY: Doubleday, 1974. The autobiography that illuminates the beliefs of a committed sixties revolutionary concerning the state of civil rights in the United States along with other issues.

I.F. Stone, *The Haunted Fifties*. New York: Random House, 1969. Columns from the visionary fifties social critic who paints a dark picture of the prevailing Cold War mentality.

Calvin Trillin, *An Education in Georgia*. Athens: University of Georgia Press, 1991. Early sixties interviews and observations by Hamilton Holmes and Charlayne Hunter describing their lives as the first black students to attend the University of Georgia in 1961.

Carolyn Wedin, *Inheritors of the Spirit*. New York: John Wiley & Sons, 1998. An autobiography of Mary White Ovington, a social activist who was a founding member of the NAACP.

Deborah Gray White, *Too Heavy a Load*. New York: W.W. Norton, 1999. Black women and their roles in the civil rights movement between 1894 and 1994.

Juan Williams, *Eyes on the Prize: America's Civil Rights Years, 1954–1965*. New York: Viking Penguin, 1987. A book about the fight for equal rights written to accompany the PBS television series of the same name.

Maxine Williams, *The Militant*. New York: Pathfinder, 1970. A pamphlet written by a member of the New York City Young Socialist Alliance and the Third World Women's Alliance concerning the role of black women in the women's liberation movement.

Miles Wolff, *Lunch at the 5 & 10*. Chicago: Elephant Paperbacks, 1990. First published in 1970, this book tells the story of the first sit-ins at the Woolworth's store in Greensboro, North Carolina, by students who successfully integrated the lunch counters throughout the South.

Periodicals

Carolyn Calloway-Thomas and Thurmon Garner, "Daisy Bates and the Little Rock Crisis: Forging the Way," *Journal of Black Studies*, 1996. An article about the woman who led the movement to integrate Central High School in 1957.

Septima Clark, "Transcript #17, Oral History Project," Atlanta: Martin Luther King Center.

Joanne Grant, "Way of Life in Mississippi," *National Guardian*, February 13, 1964. A magazine article about segregation, voting rights, and Fannie Lou Hamer's attempt to change things.

Internet Sources

J. Douglas Allen-Taylor, "Septima Clark: Teacher to a Movement," Safero, www.safero.org/articles/septima.html. A biographical article about the woman who founded the Citizenship School movement to teach voting rights to African Americans.

Sundiata Acoli, "A Brief History of the Black Panther Party and Its Place In the Black Liberation Movement," www.cs.oberlin.edu/students/pjaques/etext/acoli-hist-bpp.html, April 2, 1985.

Shirley Chisholm, "Equal Rights For Women," Gifts of Speech: Women's Speeches from Around the World, http://gos.sbc.edu/c/chisholm.html, May 21, 1969.

"Fannie Lou Hamer 1917–1977," Minerva Computer Services, 1997. www.beejae.com/hamer.htm.

Charlayne Hunter-Gault and Mary Marshall Clark, "Interview," Washington Press Club Foundation, June 15, 1993. http://womenshistory.about.com/gi/dynamic/offsite.htm?site=http%3A%2F%2Fnpc.press.org%2Fwp foral%2Fhunt1.htm.

Henry Kochlin, "We Shall Overcome," Henry's Songbook, May 6, 2002. www.mysongbook.de/msb/songs/w/weshallo.html.

Steve Levin, "Daisy Lampkin Was a Dynamo for Change," *Pittsburgh Post-Gazette*, February 2, 1998. www.post-gazette.com/blackhistory month/19980202lampkin.asp.

"Melba Pattillo Beals 1998 Interview," Scholastic, 1998. http://teacher.scholastic.com/barrier/hwyf/mpb story/melchat.htm.

Jerry Mitchell, "Rita's Story," *Mississippi Clarion-Ledger*, June 18, 2000. http://orig.clarionledger.com/news/0006/18/18msburnrita.html.

Candi Robinson, "Message to Revolutionary Women," Maoist International Movement, 2004. www.etext.org/Politics/MIM/bpp/bpp090869-23.htm.

John Simkin, "Elizabeth Eckford," Spartacus Educational (no date). www.spartacus.schoolnet.co.uk/USA eckford.htm.

"Student Nonviolent Coordinating Committee," Martin Luther King Papers Project, 2002. www.stanford.edu/group/King/about_king/encyclopedia/enc_SNCC.htm.

Index

Picture Credits

❦

About the Author

❦

Stuart A. Kallen is the author of more than 170 nonfiction books for children and young adults. He has written on topics ranging from the theory of relativity to the history of rock and roll. In addition, Mr. Kallen has written award-winning children's videos and television scripts. In his spare time, Stuart A. Kallen is a singer/song-writer/guitarist in San Diego, California.